At the Spicebox we flippin' love food!

We want to share with you our passion and knowledge
of Indian cookery and spices, to help you create
delicious food to feed your family and friends.

We have shops in Sudbury, York, Harrogate, Newcastle
and online. Pop by for tips and advice, menu planning ideas
and our handmade Curry Packs tailored to your tastes.

We also have a large range of loose spices, gift sets
and kitchenware, pickles and chutneys, snacks
and sweets, breads, rice and much more.

Whether you're a novice cook or avid foodie,
we'll have something to tickle your taste buds
and help you get creative in the kitchen.

For further information go to our website

www.spicebox.co.uk

The Spicebox family

Photography by **Jim Poyner**

© *Rafi's Spicebox Ltd, 2016*
Published by Banjara Press.

All rights reserved. No part of this book may be reproduced, adapted, stored in
a retrieval system or transmitted by any means, electronic, mechanical,
photocopying, or otherwise without prior written permission of the author.

The rights of Rafi's Spicebox Ltd to be identified as the author of this work have
been asserted in accordance with the Copyright, Designs and Patents Act 1988.

A CIP catalogue record for this book is available from the British Library.

ISBN 978-0-9956476 0 2

Book layout and cover design by:
Press Green Ltd, 20-22 Lord Mayor's Walk,
YORK YO31 7HA
www.pressgreen.com

Photography by:
Jim Poyner Photography
www.jimpoyner.co.uk

Copyediting by Pamela Hartshorne
www.pamelahartshorne.com

Prepared and printed by:
York Publishing Services Ltd,
64 Hallfield Road, York, YO31 7ZQ
www.yps-publishing.co.uk

To our Mother, Rafi, a true inspiration

CONTENTS

INTRODUCTION 10

BASICS 14

LIGHT BITES 52

THE SPICE BOX 84

MEAT & FISH 86

VEG 116

DRINKS & SWEETS 166

INDEX 192

ACKNOWLEDGEMENTS 203

INTRODUCTION

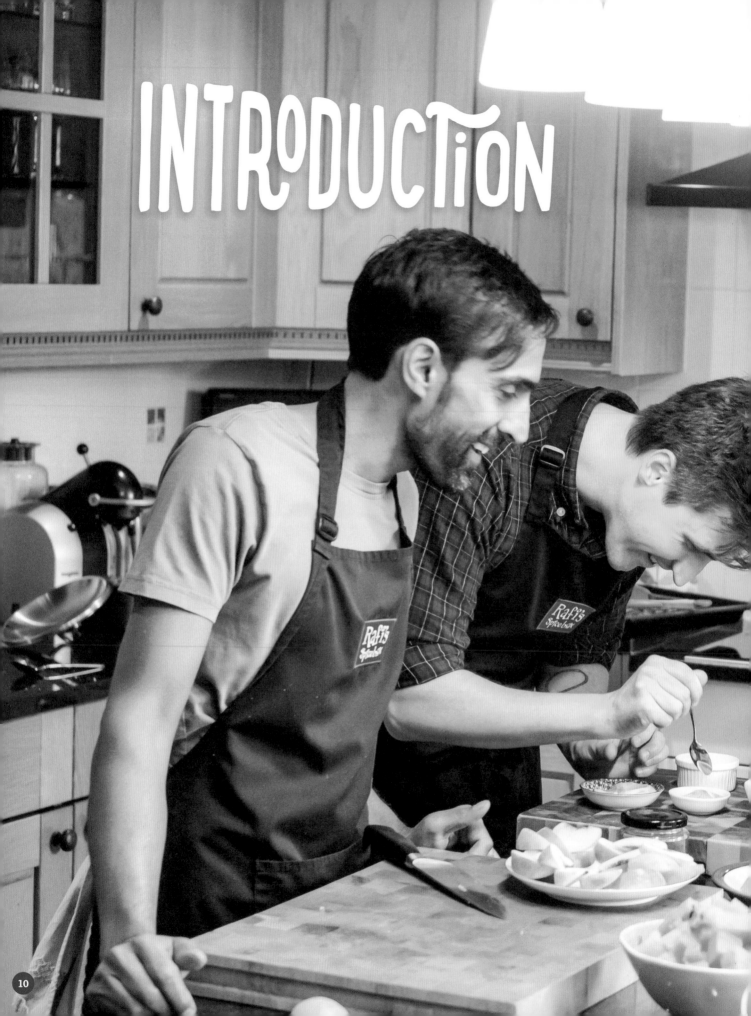

The ideas for these recipes have been bubbling away in our heads for several years now, and after much encouragement from our team and our customers, we've finally committed them to paper and released a book!

You may already know us: we're a family-run business that was set up by Rafi Fernandez in Sudbury, Suffolk. Born in Hyderabad, Rafi moved to the UK in 1965, and after writing several brilliant cookbooks she set up her first Spicebox shop in 1989. She passed on her cooking skills and experience to her sons, Kevin and Lee, along with the rest of her team of foodies, and her recipes and her love of sharing her knowledge have been an inspiration to us, especially when writing this book.

Rafi's aim always was, and ours still is, to inspire you to cook the best food that you can. If we can encourage you to enjoy the whole process of cooking these dishes and sharing them with family or with friends, our work is done.

As you're holding this book, we're already halfway there. You are obviously curious about spices and willing to learn, we have lots of knowledge and ideas that we can't wait to share with you!

Here's a few points to note before we get started:

First, you need quality ingredients. This means using some of the lovely produce that we get here in the UK, ideally when it is in season and when it is fresh. That also means using quality spices, buying whole spices and in smaller quantities so they keep their amazing flavours until they are needed. For more tips on spices *see page 84*.

Next, make the food you cook fit in with the lifestyle you lead. If you want food that can be prepared quickly, we can help you with that. If you want to spend a little more time before hosting an impressive dinner party, we can help you with that too. Do you only eat vegetarian food? No problem. Once you understand what you enjoy cooking (which is just as important as the finished result!), it is easier for you to find recipes to suit your style and your time constraints. We've covered all bases in this book.

Finally, we think confidence is really important when it comes to good food. Indian food is not only delicious, it is very adaptable. If you don't have a certain ingredient or if you don't like it, simply leave it out or swap it for something you do have. We hope the notes and tips in the following pages really help you gain some confidence in your own cooking. Feeling assured in the kitchen makes the whole process so much more enjoyable, and it gives you the freedom to experiment with different flavours and combinations.

The recipes in this book are all based on Indian flavours and concepts, but we have given them a twist of our own. We've adapted them to work with ingredients that are readily available in the UK, and to fit in with the British way of life. We have plenty of recipes that would work brilliantly as part of a Sunday roast and others that would make a drizzly British barbecue particularly delicious. Some of them have evolved from Rafi's original recipes, some have been inspired by the team's travels and own tastes. Whatever their starting point, we're very proud of these dishes, and hope to hear what you've done with them in your own kitchen!

We hope you love this book as much as we do.

As Rafi would say...

'SANJOG BHOJAN' (happy dining)

BASICS

Indian food is famous for its delicious breads, rice and chutneys, these recipes add flair and variety to any dish. We've called them basics as they would be prepared for every meal, but they are big on flavour and can really turn a spread into something special. ■

ACHAR
(Malaysian Mixed Vegetable Pickle)

Vegan V Vegetarian
Gluten free Makes 6 jars

This is one of Rafi's classic recipes from her first book *Malaysian Cookery*, written in 1985. She would make this pickle up in large quantities and give it to the family as gifts. It is a great combination of hot, sweet, tart and crunchy vegetables that is perfect with any Asian meal - or in a ham and cheese sandwich!

Ingredients

1 pint pickling vinegar

300g carrots, peeled and cut into 5 cm batons

300g cauliflower, cut into florets

300g white cabbage, cut into 1 cm strips

300g cucumber, deseeded and cut into 5cm batons

2 fresh red chillies, slit lengthways (optional)

250g demerara sugar

275g salted peanuts, coarsely ground in a coffee grinder or bashed in a tea towel

175g sesame seeds, dry roasted until golden brown

1 ½ tsp turmeric

2 tbsp chilli powder (less if a milder version required)

150ml vegetable oil

5 cloves garlic, finely minced

1 tsp salt

Method

1. Bring the vinegar to the boil in a large saucepan and blanch each vegetable at a time for 30 seconds. Discard the vinegar.

2. Once all vegetables are blanched and well drained, combine in a large bowl.

3. Add the sugar, peanuts and sesame seeds and toss well.

4. Mix the turmeric and chilli powder with a little water to form a thin paste.

5. Heat the oil in a large frying pan and gently fry the garlic cloves over a medium heat until fragrant but not coloured.

6. Add the chilli and turmeric paste and salt and fry well for at least 5 minutes. Remove from the heat and cool.

7. Once completely cool, add to the vegetables and mix thoroughly.

8. Store in sterilised jars.

BEETROOT PICKLE

V Vegetarian Vegan Gluten free Makes 1 large jar

This is a light, but earthy pickle, it adds great colour and texture to any meal. It's also really nice served simply with cheese. It will not last as long as other pickles, but definitely improves in flavour after a few days.

Ingredients

500g raw beetroot, grated

1 tsp salt

1 tsp sugar

1 tsp coriander seeds

1 tsp fennel seeds

2 tbsp vegetable oil

1 tsp mustard seeds

½ tsp cumin seeds

1 red onion, finely sliced

1-2 tsp of chilli flakes we like to use pul biber (p. 155), which is slightly milder

40ml of cider vinegar

2 cloves of garlic, minced

1 inch piece ginger, minced

Method

1. In a bowl mix the beetroot with the salt and sugar and leave to rest for 30 minutes.

2. Toast the coriander seeds and fennel seeds in a dry pan for 1-2 minutes, allow to cool and then grind to a coarse powder.

3. Heat the oil in a frying pan and add the mustard seeds and cumin seeds. Cook for 1-2 minutes until the mustard seeds start popping.

4. Turn the heat down and gently fry the onion for 15 minutes.

5. Add the ground coriander and fennel and the chilli flakes, mix together and cook for 1 minute. Remove the mix from the pan and allow it to cool.

6. Add the onion mixture, vinegar, garlic and ginger to the beetroot. Mix everything together for 3-4 minutes, to release a little liquid from the beetroot.

7. Cover and leave to sit at room temperature for 24 hours before serving. Any leftovers can be put in a clean jar and will last in the fridge for 2-3 weeks.

Alternatives:
Could use grated carrots instead of beetroot.

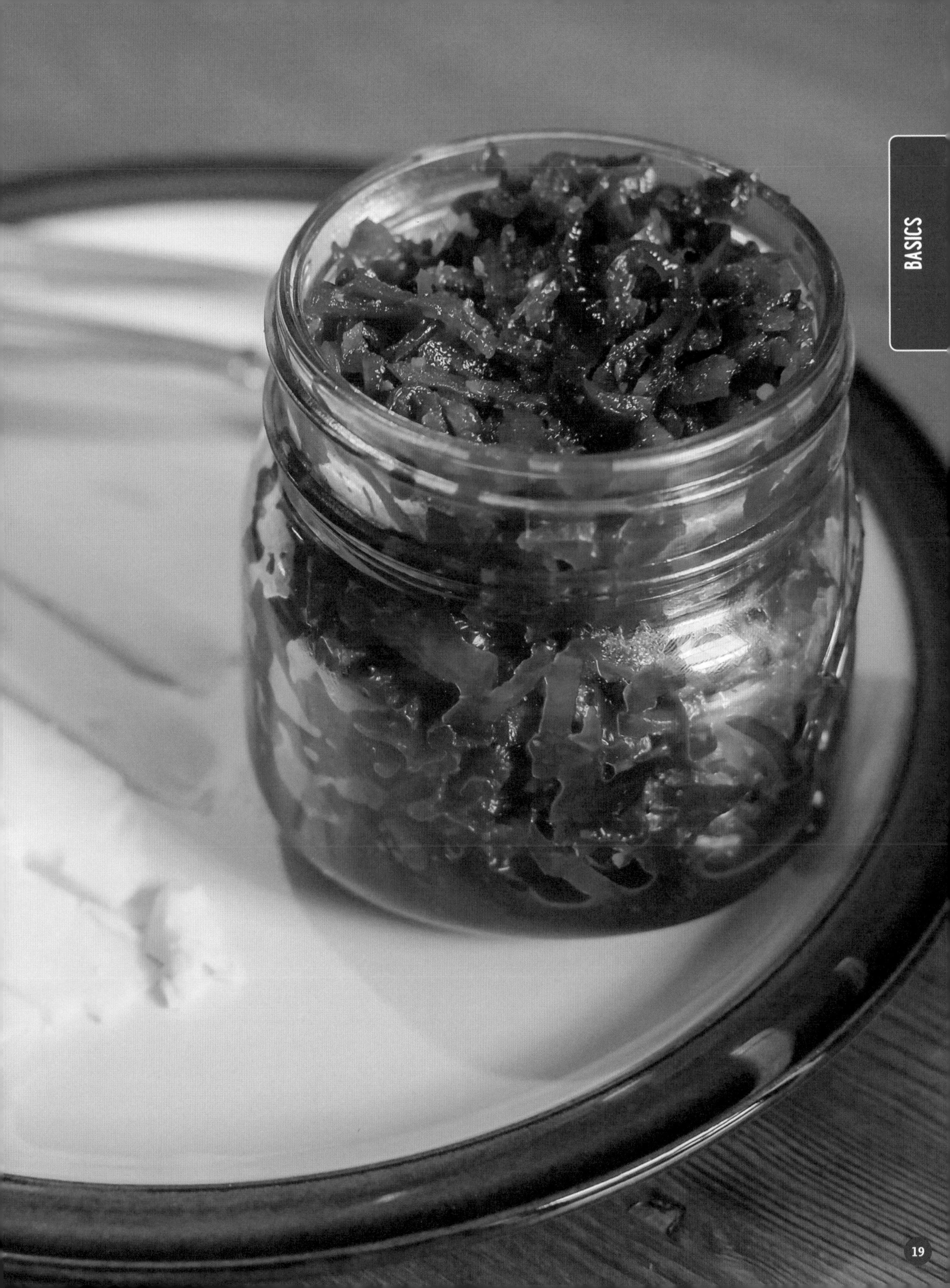

CHAPATI (Flatbread)

Ⓥ Vegetarian 👽 Vegan 👥 Makes roughly 12-15 breads

These breads are made every day in India, and are served with everything. They're great for scooping up wet dishes, such as dahls, or using as a wrap for barbecued meats.

Rafi was told when she was learning to make chapatis that they should be "as round as the world, not in different shapes of its continents!" We don't really mind if our flatbreads aren't completely round (they are still delicious!), but the best advice to get perfect discs is to practice making them for breakfast, lunch and dinner every day!

Ingredients

500g chapati flour
(or 450g white flour and
50g wholemeal)

Pinch of salt

1 tbsp vegetable oil

300g warm water (approx)

Small bowl of flour to
use when rolling out

Mixing the dough

1. Mix the flour and the salt. Pour in the oil and rub with your fingers- like making pastry - until it is evenly combined with the flour.

2. Start adding in the water, bit by bit, to form a soft dough, which is fully combined with no dry bits and slightly tacky. Don't worry if it is still sticking to your hands slightly.

3. Cover the bowl with a damp tea towel or a (unused!) shower cap, and leave the dough to rest for 15 minutes.

4. Turn the dough out onto a clean work surface and knead briefly for 4-5 minutes. Try and avoid adding any more flour at this stage. Once kneaded, the dough should be soft and smooth. It may still be a little sticky, but you should notice that it is much less tacky than when you first mixed the dough.

5. Cover the bowl and leave to rest again for 30-40 minutes. This resting period is very important, as the flour will continue to absorb moisture from the liquid and it allows the dough to relax, becoming more elastic.

Shaping the dough

1. Turn the dough out again (you should notice now that it is less sticky and easier to handle, as well as being lovely and soft). Divide the dough into about 12-15 balls (depending on the size you want), rolling them between your hands. Cover these with your towel or, if it is big enough, you could use your upturned bowl. This stops the balls from drying out and forming a skin whilst you are rolling and cooking the breads.

2. Take the first ball and dip it all over in the bowl of flour, gently pat off any excess flour. Flatten the ball between the hands into a disc shape.

3. On the work top, give the dough a couple of rolls forward and back using a rolling pin, then give the dough a quarter turn and repeat. Leave it to rest for 30 seconds – 1 minute and then repeat the action. Depending on how thick or thin you want your breads, this action could be repeated again. (If possible try not to add any more flour at this stage; if it feels like it's going to stick, give a light dusting over the dough or on your rolling pin).

Cooking the dough

1. Heat a frying pan until it is nice and hot, then turn down to medium-hot heat.

2. Dust off any excess flour (as this can burn when cooking) and carefully lay the rolled-out dough in the pan.

3. Cook for 1-2 minutes until bubbles start to form on the surface. Turn it over and cook the other side for a further 1-2 minutes. Use a spatula to press the edges to encourage it to puff and get steam inside the bread. Give it another turn and cook briefly, making sure there are no uncooked bits of dough.

4. Remove from the pan and either wrap in a clean tea towel or cover with foil to keep warm.

5. Repeat the process with the rest of the dough balls.

Top Tip:

You may not need all the water or you may need a little more. This all depends on the type/quality of the flour you are using, the temperature of the water and the temperature/humidity of your house.

Trying not to add much excess flour and keeping a soft dough will result in softer, tastier flatbreads.

CHERRY TOMATO CHUTNEY

V Vegetarian   Vegan

Gluten free   Makes 2 jars

This chutney makes a nice condiment for any meal or could even be used in sandwiches or with a cheese board. It will last in the fridge for at least a week, and is a good accompaniment to make up in advance.

Ingredients

2 tbsp vegetable oil

1 tsp panch pooran

1 onion, diced

2 cloves of garlic, finely sliced

1 red chilli, finely sliced (optional)

¼ tsp turmeric

400g cherry tomatoes, halved

20g jaggery (p. 170), grated or cut into small pieces

2 tbsp white wine vinegar

Salt, to taste

Method

1. Heat the oil to a medium heat in a saucepan and fry the panch pooran spices for 1-2 minutes.

2. Add the onion, garlic, chilli and gently fry for 4-5 minutes, until softened.

3. Add the turmeric, mix with the onions and then add the tomatoes.

4. Add the jaggery and vinegar and mix well. Cover with a lid and leave to cook for 10 minutes.

5. Remove the lid and give it a mix. Turn up the heat and cook for a further 2-3 minutes to remove any excess liquid.

6. Season with salt, to taste. Leave to cool to room temperature before serving.

Spice Notes:

Panch pooran is a Bengali five-spice mix with equal parts cumin seeds, mustard seeds, fenugreek seeds, onion seeds and fennel seeds. It's a very versatile blend which can be used in any vegetable stir fry.

CHILLI SAMBAL

Ⓥ Vegetarian   🌱 Vegan   🌾 Gluten free   👥 Makes 1 jar

"I always have a jar of this in the fridge, and I use this hot relish on burgers, with chips, alongside milder curries or as a base for a pasta sauce. Its bright colour and strong flavour really perk up any meal!" – *Hana*

Ingredients

20g of dried red chillies, soaked in 150ml of just-boiled water for 10 minutes

2 cloves of garlic, peeled

2 fresh red chillies, stalks removed

4 tsp white wine vinegar

2 tsp salt

4 tsp sugar

Method

1. Blend all the ingredients together, including the water used to soak the chillies.

2. Adjust to taste, adding more salt, sugar or garlic.

Alternatives:
Other dried chillies will work well with this, all affecting the final flavour and heat strength of the sauce. Try using chipotles for a Mexican style sauce, or habanero for a more Caribbean influence.

LEE'S COCONUT CHUTNEY

V Vegetarian · Vegan
Gluten free · Makes 1 jar

One of the most important condiments in South India, this is served at all meals of the day, particularly with dosas, idlis and sambhar. Many communities have their own version; this is Lee's recipe that he found whilst travelling in Mysore and Kerala. He has been on a mission for many years to discover the best recipe and he says that this is not only the tastiest but also the simplest to make.

Ingredients

100g desiccated coconut

1 tbsp urid dhal (lentil), soaked overnight

1 green chilli

Handful of fresh coriander

½ tsp salt

Water

1 tbsp vegetable oil

6 curry leaves

1 tsp mustard seeds

1 dry red chilli

Method

1. In a food processor, blend the drained lentils, coconut, green chilli and coriander with a little water until you achieve a single cream consistency.

2. Heat the vegetable oil in a small frying pan and add the curry leaves, mustard seeds and dry red chilli and fry for 5 minutes until the chilli is dark. Set aside and cool.

3. Combine the coconut mixture with the fried seeds and season to taste.

Top Tip:
"This can, and probably should, be served with everything!" - Lee

COCONUT RICE

V Vegetarian · Vegan · Gluten free · Serves 4-6 people

This is a typical South Indian rice preparation. It works well with all Indian food, but is particularly delicious with seafood.

Ingredients

300g basmati rice

2 tbsp coconut oil

1 tsp mustard seeds

1 tbsp urid dhal (lentil)

1 tbsp chana dhal (lentil)

1 dry red chilli

8 fresh curry leaves

12 cashew nuts

Pinch asafoetida

1 green chilli, slit lengthways

1 tbsp grated ginger

100g creamed coconut

Salt to taste

Method

1. Cook the rice using the instructions for plain rice *(p. 40)* or use leftover rice.

2. Heat the coconut oil in a large frying pan and fry the mustard seeds, lentils, dry chilli, curry leaves and cashew nuts until the seeds pop and the nuts turn golden brown.

3. Add the creamed coconut, asafoetida, ginger and chilli and fry for a further 3-4 minutes.

4. Add the rice and continue to stir over a medium heat to warm through.

5. Season with salt to taste and serve piping hot.

CORIANDER CHUTNEY

(V) Vegetarian (🌱) Vegan (🌾) Gluten free (👥) Makes 1 jar

This fresh herb condiment is a traditional accompaniment to a lot of snack foods and is delicious with all Indian dishes. It can also be stirred through yoghurt to make a raita, or used as a marinade for prawns.

Ingredients

1 green chilli

10g fresh ginger, peeled

100g fresh coriander (leaves and stalks)

10g desiccated coconut

Juice of 1 lemon

½ tsp ground cumin

Pinch of salt

Pinch of sugar

Method

1. Put all the ingredients in a blender (or use a stick blender) and blitz together with a splash of water until smooth.

2. Adjust salt, sugar and lemon juice to taste.

Top Tip:
Try substituting some of the coriander with fresh mint.

LEMON RICE

V Vegetarian Vegan Gluten free Serves 4-6 people

This rice dish has loads of textures and bright flavours and is delicious alongside vegetable dishes. The original recipe comes from a lady called Laxmi, whom Lee met on his travels in India.

Ingredients

300g basmati rice

2 tbsp vegetable oil

¼ tsp mustard seeds

8 fresh curry leaves

3 tsp chana dhal (lentil)

1 ½ tsp urid dhal (lentil)

2 tbsp of peanuts (skin on)

1 tbsp cashews

½ tsp turmeric

1 lemon

Chopped coriander to taste

Method

1. Cook and cool the rice, as per the plain rice instructions *(p. 40)*, leave to rest for 20 minutes.

2. Heat the oil over a low to medium heat, gently fry the seeds, curry leaves and lentils slowly for 10 minutes. until the lentils are golden brown and the spices are fragrant.

3. Add the nuts to the pan and continue to fry till the nuts are golden being careful not to burn the spices.

4. Take off the heat and add the turmeric and let sizzle, then allow the mixture to cool.

5. Add this to the rice along with the lemon juice and chopped coriander. Season and serve, best eaten at room temperature.

Top Tip:
Microwave the lemon for 10 seconds, and then roll it on the work surface before juicing it to help release more juice.

NAAN BREADS

(V) Vegetarian (👥) Makes 8-10 naan breads

These traditional breads are delicious served alongside all meals. Traditionally cooked in a tandoor oven, this recipe can be cooked in a hot frying pan or on the barbecue.

The long slow proving of the dough helps to develop both the flavour and the texture of the breads. It also makes it much easier to plan making the breads around other things. You could, for example, mix the dough first thing in the morning, stick it in the fridge, and then cook the breads later in the evening for dinner. Or mix the dough before going to bed and then cook the breads in the morning or afternoon the following day.

Ingredients

300ml milk, room temperature

2g dried yeast

1 tsp sugar

20g yoghurt

500g strong bread flour

1 tsp salt

20g melted butter, plus more to spread over naans once cooked

Top Tips:
Try adding 1 tsp of onion seeds or some fresh coriander to the dough when mixing it.

Try adding a little crushed garlic to the melted butter used to spread over the cooked naan breads.

For Peshwari naans, add 2 tbsp of ground almonds and a handful of sultanas to the dough when mixing.

Method

1. In a large bowl add the milk, yoghurt, sugar and yeast. Stir until everything is combined and the yeast has dissolved.

2. Add the flour and the salt on top of the ingredients in the bowl and, using your fingers, mix the salt through the flour.

3. Add the melted butter and then mix the dough together, so there are no dry bits.

4. Cover the bowl with cling film or a damp tea towel and leave to rest for 20 minutes.

5. Tip the dough on to a work top and knead for about 4-5 minutes.

6. Shape the dough in to a ball, put it back in the bowl or a large Tupperware container, cover and then transfer the dough to the fridge.

7. The dough can now be left to rise slowly for 8-12 hours.

8. When you're ready to make the naan breads, remove the dough from the fridge and place on a lightly dusted work top. Divide the dough and shape into balls (8-12 balls depending on the size of naan bread you would like). Leave the dough balls to rest (covered) for 10-15 minutes.

9. Heat a large frying pan until nice and hot.

10. Roll out one of the dough balls into a round (or tear drop shape) with a light dusting of flour. Tap off any excess flour and then transfer to the dry frying pan.

11. Cook the naan bread for 3-4 minutes each side until cooked. Check that there are no uncooked doughy bits on the surface.

12. Remove from the pan and if you want, spread over a little bit of melted butter. Wrap in foil to keep warm while cooking the other breads.

PARATHA (Layered Flatbreads)

 Vegetarian Vegan 👥 Makes 10-12 parathas

Paratha are another form of flatbreads, but they are layered to provide a flaky, rich texture. They are wonderful with absolutely anything, but often served with vegetable dishes.

Ingredients

1 quantity of basic chapati dough *(p. 20)*

Small amount of flour

Small bowl of vegetable oil (plus pastry brush)

Top Tip:
For extra richness, you could use melted butter to brush the dough before folding.

Shaping the dough

1. Divide the dough into balls, as in the basic chapati recipe.

2. Brush a little oil on the work surface. Flatten the ball into a disk.

3. Rub a little oil onto the rolling pin and roll the dough into a large thin sheet (it doesn't matter at this stage if it isn't completely round).

4. Brush some more oil over the surface of the dough and sprinkle with a little bit of flour.

5. Starting at the end nearest you, lift the edge of the dough. Peel it away from you and then back towards you, folding the dough to create a 'z' shape fold. This fold should be about 2 inches wide. Repeat the process, but this time picking up the folded portion. Continue this way until you have a strip of dough with a concertina fold all the way through.

6. Holding the two ends, give the dough a gentle stretch, and then from one end, start rolling up the strip into a spiral shape. When completely rolled, tuck outer end underneath. Put this rolled spiral to one side and cover. Repeat the process with the other balls of dough.

Rolling the dough

1. Brush a little more oil on to the surface. Gently press the spiralled dough into a disc and then carefully roll into a circle. To keep the layers, work gently and don't roll the dough quite as thin as for chapatis.

2. As with the basic chapatis, you can get into a rhythm rolling out the next paratha while one is cooking.

Cooking the dough

1. Cook the dough in a hot frying pan, 2-3 minutes each side. Before turning, brush a little more oil on to the surface of the dough. There shouldn't be any raw bits of dough and it should be nice and golden.

2. Stack in a clean towel or under foil to keep warm while cooking the other dough spirals.

PICKLED ONIONS

(V) Vegetarian   (🌾) Gluten free

(🌱) Vegan   (👥) Serves 4 as an accompaniment

"I love mixing these pickled onions into a whole plate of Indian food to provide little pops of sharpness and crunch. They also add vibrancy and texture to salads, or to barbecued meat in a wrap." — *Hana*

Ingredients

2 finely diced red onions

2 tbsp acid of your choice - lemon juice, lime juice, cider vinegar, white wine vinegar or balsamic are all good options

Handful of finely sliced fresh coriander

1 tsp salt

1 tsp sugar

Method

1. Mix all ingredients together.
2. Chill for an hour or so (or overnight)
3. Serve alongside anything!

PLAIN RICE

(V) Vegetarian (🌱) Vegan (🌾) Gluten free (👥) Serves 4 people

"Rice is a really important part of our cuisine and it should be given as much thought and time as the main and side dishes you prepare. We are often told that people have difficulty with rice and therefore resort to using pre-cooked or easy cook versions. Once you have mastered the technique below you should be able to ensure that you always have good quality, well cooked rice as part of your meal and understand the importance of it through the amazing taste and texture you achieve.

Rafi was particularly passionate about rice. Being from South India, it formed an important part of her diet and could easily feature in all three meals of the day in some form. As a child it was always my responsibility to cook the rice for our family meals and while I always found it a chore, the process has stuck with me and I now cook it almost instinctively without thinking.

The key here is to measure the ingredients correctly. I always use the cup pictured, which is the same style of cup I used as a child. It holds approximately 150g rice and this is enough for 2 people. The other important point is not to remove the lid during cooking as it will release the essential steam produced. My mother always reminded me that if I did remove the lid the 'Rice God' would punish me: I don't know how true this is, but I was always too scared to try." – *Kevin*

Ingredients

300g basmati rice

500ml cold water

Salt to taste

Method

1. Add all the ingredients to a saucepan with a tight-fitting lid and bring to the boil.

2. As soon as it starts to boil cover tightly with the lid and reduce the heat to the lowest possible setting and cook for exactly 12 minutes.

3. After 12 minutes, remove from the heat and leave to rest for a further 3 minutes.

4. The rice is now ready. Simply fluff up the grains gently with a fork to serve.

Alternatives:
For a simple fragrant pilau, gently fry fragrant spices like cloves, cardamom and cinnamon in 1 tbsp of butter for 3–4 minutes before adding the rice and follow the same method as above.

PUDLAS
(Gujarati Gram Flour Pancakes)

Vegan · Gluten free · Serves 4 people

A simple Gujarati pancake which is traditionally served for breakfast, although they also make an ideal brunch or a light lunch. These are best eaten fresh with a simple vegetable dish and dhal.

Ingredients

225g gram flour

1 onion, grated

½ tsp ajwain seeds

¼ tsp asafoetida

Pinch of salt

375ml of water

Oil for frying

Method

1. Add the gram flour to a bowl and whisk to remove any large lumps.

2. Add the onion, ajwain, asafoetida and salt and mix.

3. Add the water slowly to prevent lumps and whisk everything together.

4. When everything is combined you should have quite a thin batter. Cover and leave to rest for 30 minutes.

5. Heat a small frying pan and when hot, add a little oil. Pour in one ladle of the batter and swirl around the pan (just like pancake day!). Let it cook for 1-2 minutes until the top has just set. The underneath should be golden and should come away from the pan. Flip it over and cook the other side for another 1-2 minutes.

6. Remove from the pan and wrap in some foil to keep warm.

7. Repeat the process with the rest of batter, adding a drop of oil between each pancake, to stop them sticking.

Top Tip:
You can also add grated tomato or fresh chilli to the batter.

STUFFED PARATHAS

These breads are a fantastic way of using up any leftovers you may have. The spiced mashed potato *(p. 156)* or the kheema *(p. 105)* both work beautifully as fillings.

Ingredients

1 quantity of basic chapati dough *(p. 20)*

Small bowl of flour

Oil for brushing

Leftover keema or spiced mash potato (roughly 2 tbsp per paratha)

Method

1. Divide and roll the dough into 12 balls, set aside and cover.

2. Take a dough ball dip it in the flour and pat off any excess. Flatten the ball into a disk and roll out a little, forming a small circle of dough. Give an extra small roll around the outer edge so it is slightly thinner than the middle.

3. Put 1-2 tbsp of your filling in the centre of the dough.

4. Fold in the outer edges to all meet in the middle, and squeeze the edges together to seal.

5. Dip the stuffed dough in the flour again and pat off any excess. Roll out into a round: you should be able to see the filling through the dough, but try not to let it tear.

6. Brush the upper side with oil and turn oil side down into a hot pan. Cook for 2-3 minutes each side, brushing the top side with little oil before turning. It's ready when it is golden and there are no raw bits of dough.

7. Spread with a bit of butter and serve hot.

Alternatives:
Onions lightly fried with cumin seeds and fresh coriander. Brussel sprouts *(p. 127)* spinach and onions *(p. 160)*.

TARKA YOGHURT

(V) Vegetarian (✻) Gluten free (👥) Makes 1 bowl

This is a recipe from Rafi's *Indian Vegetarian Cookery* from 1986. We often take it to parties as a dip for crisps and crudités as it is quite unusual. It's also great served alongside any Indian inspired meal.

We always serve yoghurt in some form with an Indian meal as it helps neutralise any excessive heat from chillies as well as aiding digestion.

Ingredients

1 tub natural yoghurt (500g)

¼ tsp salt

For the tarka:

4 tbsp vegetable oil

1 dried red chilli

¼ tsp mustard seeds

¼ tsp cumin seeds

4 curry leaves

¼ tsp asafoetida

¼ tsp turmeric

Method

1 Mix the yoghurt with the salt.

2 Heat the oil in a small pan. Fry all the tarka ingredients gently for 1-2 minutes.

3 Immediately pour the spices and oil over the yoghurt and cover with a lid.

4 Stir through before serving.

Top Tip:
The tarka (tempering of spices) is a great technique to master as it can turn any ordinary dish especially leftovers into something amazing. When you have perfected the tarka the spices can vary depending on your taste or mood.

Alternatives:
If you want, you can also stir some fresh herbs through the yoghurt or add garlic to the fry.

SOUTH INDIAN TOMATO RICE

(V) Vegetarian 🌱 Vegan 🌾 Gluten free 👥 Serves 4-6 people

This spiced, flavourful rice is the perfect accompaniment to a fish dish, or can be served on its own for a light lunch with some yoghurt or raita.

Ingredients

300g basmati rice

1 tsp chana dhal (lentils)

1 tsp coriander seeds

1 dry red chilli, broken into pieces

2 tbsp vegetable oil

6-8 curry leaves, finely sliced.

½ tsp mustard seeds

¼ tsp asafoetida

1 onion, diced

4 tomatoes, diced

Salt, to taste

Method

1. Cook the rice as per the plain rice recipe (p. 40).

2. In a dry pan, toast the coriander seed, chana dhal and dry red chilli for 1-2 minutes until golden. Remove from the pan and leave to cool. Once cool, grind to a fine powder using either a pestle and mortar or a coffee grinder.

3. Heat the oil in a frying pan and fry the curry leaves, mustard seeds and asafoetida for 1-2 minutes.

4. Add the onion and fry for 5 minutes.

5. Add the tomatoes and fry for 10 minutes until they are soft and most of the liquid has evaporated.

6. Stir in the ground ingredients and take off the heat.

7. Mix in all of the cooked rice and season with salt, to taste.

Top Tip:
This dish has a bit of heat from the dry chilli, which can be omitted. For an earthy flavour, try adding 1 tsp of urid dhal (lentils) to the mix to be ground.

VEGETABLE PILAU

(V) Vegetarian (🌾) Gluten free (👥) Serves 4-6 people

This is often served as part of a large banquet during the Muslim festival of Ramadan. Rafi always used to serve her egg curry *(p. 127)* with a rice dish like this.

Ingredients

500g mixed vegetables such as carrots, green beans, cauliflower and sweetcorn

50g butter

4 cloves garlic, finely chopped

1 inch ginger, finely grated

2 green chillies, finely chopped, deseeded if preferred

1 inch cinnamon bark

½ tsp black cumin

3 cloves

½ tsp turmeric

½ tsp garam masala

300g basmati rice

50g cashew nuts

50g almonds

Salt

1 litre water

Method

1. Cut all the vegetables into small bite sized pieces and blanch them for 1 minute in salted water.

2. Drain and keep aside.

3. In a large pan with a tight fitting lid, heat the butter and lightly fry the garlic, ginger, chillies and spices for 2 to 3 minutes.

4. Add the vegetables, rice and nuts and mix thoroughly, season with salt to taste and add the water.

5. Bring to the boil, cover with a piece of foil and the lid and reduce the heat to the lowest setting. Cook for 15 minutes: remove from the heat and leave to stand for 2 minutes before serving.

LIGHT BITES

This chapter has been inspired by Indian street-food, which is vibrant, quick to cook and easy to eat. While all these dishes can be eaten as a snack, they also make delicious light lunch options, or can form part of a spicy picnic. ∎

LEE'S ALOO CHAAT
Mix the potato chaat with
a handful of toasted mixed
seeds and fresh cress.

IAN'S ALOO CHAAT
Mix the potato chaat with
finely chopped red onion and
chopped tomato and a good
squeeze of lemon juice.

HANA'S ALOO CHAAT
Mix the potato chaat with
chopped spring onion
and chopped fresh mint.

ALOO CHAAT
(Potato Snack)

(V) Vegetarian (🌱) Vegan (🌾) Gluten free (👥) Serves 4-6 People

We love these chaats (snacks) here at the Spicebox: they're a staff lunch staple! They are often tangy, sour, salty, a little sweet, with loads of different textures. It's so easy for each person to build their own perfect snack by mixing individual portions from the ingredients. There is no equivalent snack here in the UK!

This recipe is a great starting point for lots of different styles of chaat. You can eat the potatoes as they are, or add things into the mix for different textures and flavours.

Ingredients

1kg potatoes, peeled and diced

2-3 tbsp vegetable oil

2 tsp ground cumin

2-3 tsp chaat masala, to taste

2 tsp amchur powder (mango powder)

¼ tsp chilli powder

Salt to taste

To garnish – a squeeze of lemon juice and fresh chopped coriander

DEFINITION:

Chaat is a term used in India to describe a savoury snack, often served as a street food. Chaat Masala is a unique salty, tangy blend of spices often used as a garnish.

Method

1. Pre-heat the oven to 240C/gas 9.

2. Put the potatoes on a large roasting tray, drizzle over the oil and roast in the oven for about 30 minutes (stirring after 15 minutes) until they are cooked through and starting to crisp up.

3. Remove from the oven, and allow to cool.

4. Mix the potatoes with the remaining ingredients. Adjust to taste by adding more chaat masala and/or salt.

5. Garnish with a squeeze of lemon juice and fresh coriander.

Top Tip:

Use tinned chickpeas instead of roasted potatoes. This makes an incredibly quick and healthy dish!

Alternatives:

There's an endless list of things you can try adding to this tasty snack: Bombay mix, peanuts, seeds, grated carrots, shredded red cabbage, cucumber, yoghurt, tamarind chutney, fresh coriander, mint, fresh peas... Get experimenting until you find your perfect chaat!

ASPARAGUS DIPPERS, BOILED EGGS AND SPICED SALTS

(V) Vegetarian (🌾) Gluten free (👥) Serves 4 people

A twist on the traditional eggs and toast soldiers. Using asparagus in season and spicy salts really ups the ante for a delicious and healthy brunch. You'll be fighting over them - we certainly do!

Ingredients

250g asparagus

1 tbsp vegetable oil

4 eggs

Spiced salts options:

1. 2 tsp toasted cumin seeds ground together with 1 tsp of sea salt flakes

2. 1 tsp of chilli flakes mixed with ½ tsp sea salt flakes

3. Grind together ½ tsp black peppercorns, ½ tsp sea salt flakes and then stir through ½ tsp amchur powder (mango powder)

Method

1. Cook the eggs in boiling water for 5-6 minutes for soft boiled eggs.

2. Drizzle oil over the asparagus and cook in a very hot pan or using a griddle pan for 4-6 minutes (depending on the thickness of the spears).

3. Serve the egg in an egg cup, dip in the asparagus spears and sprinkle with one of the spiced salts.

BARBECUED SWEETCORN WITH LIME AND CHAAT

(V) Vegetarian (🌱) Vegan (🌾) Gluten free (👥) Serves 4 people

This recipe has been a revelation to us: we can't eat plain corn on the cob ever again! In India, the corn is often cooked straight in the ashes of the fire, to help pick up a really smoky flavour. We use a barbecue to achieve a similar result. It's messy to eat, but it's so worth it!

Ingredients

4 corn on the cob (husks removed)

1 lime, cut into wedges

4 tsp chaat masala (p. 55)

Method

1. Microwave the corn on high for 3-4 minutes to soften slightly.

2. Transfer to a barbecue or grill and finish cooking until the corn has picked up some colour.

3. To serve, dip the wedge of lime into the chaat masala and then rub and squish the lime juice and chaat all over the corn.

BHEL PURI

Ⓥ Vegetarian 🌱 Vegan 👥 Serves 6 people as a snack

Bhel puri is a popular street food snack in India and it has many varieties. This is brilliant for experimenting with different flavours and textures - there is no right or wrong in this dish, just hot, sweet, crunchy, soft deliciousness!

Lovely served as a snack or for a light lunch.

Ingredients

1 onion, finely diced

1 lemon

150g boiled potatoes, cubed

1-2 tsp chaat masala *(p. 55)*

Handful of fresh coriander, chopped

2 large tomatoes, diced

150g bhel puri mix

2-3 tbsp tamarind chutney (to taste). We use *Geeta's Tamarind Chutney*, let down with a little hot water so it's runny

1-2 tbsp coriander chutney *(p. 31)*

Method

1. In a bowl mix the onions with the lemon juice and leave to rest for at least 10 minutes.

2. Empty Bhel Puri mix in to a large bowl. Add the onions, potatoes, chaat masala, fresh coriander, tomatoes and chutneys and mix thoroughly.

3. Eat straight away. Then go back for seconds!

Top Tip:
Bhel puri mixes usually contain a combination of lightly flavoured puffed rice, nuts and other crunchy bits made from wheat flour and chickpea flour. If you can't find this any good quality Bombay mix will do.

CHICKPEA CHAAT
(Chickpea Salad)

(V) Vegetarian (🌱) Vegan (🌾) Gluten free (👥) Serves 4-6 people

This dish is nice for a summer buffet or as part of a light lunch. It can also be served alongside grilled meat, and can be easily customised by including different vegetables.

Ingredients

2 x 400g tins of chickpeas, drained and rinsed

1 carrot, grated

1 red onion, finely chopped

Juice of 1 lemon

1 tbsp of olive oil

1 tsp cumin seeds

1 tsp onion seeds

Handful of fresh coriander, chopped

1 tbsp of tamarind chutney. We use *Geeta's Tamarind Chutney*, let down with a little hot water so it's runny

Salt, to taste

Sev to garnish (optional)

Method

1. Mix together the chickpeas, carrot, onion and lemon juice.

2. In a small frying pan, heat the oil and fry the cumin and onion seeds for 1-2 minutes until the cumin seeds start to brown. Pour this over the chickpeas and stir in.

3. Add the tamarind chutney, coriander and salt and mix well. Give it a taste and add more chutney/coriander/salt to suit your tastes.

4. Sprinkle generously with sev just before serving.

Note:
Sev is a traditional Indian snack consisting of long thin strands made from gram flour, fried and lightly spiced. They can be found in good Asian grocers.

COURGETTE KOFTAS

(V) Vegetarian (🌱) Vegan (🌾) Gluten free (👥) Makes 8

These vegetable koftas are often made in India with bottlegourd, but here we have used courgettes which grow in abundance in the UK during the summer. They can be served as a snack, or alongside other dishes. These work really well added to kadhi, a yoghurt curry sauce *(p. 140)*.

Ingredients

2 courgettes (500g), coarsely grated

1 onion, coarsely grated

2 cloves of garlic, finely grated

1 inch ginger

Pinch of salt

½ tsp turmeric

1 ½ tsp garam masala

50g gram flour (approx.)

Method

1. Put the courgettes in a sieve, sprinkle with a little salt and leave for 10 minutes. Squeeze with your hands to remove as much liquid as you can.

2. Put the drained courgettes into a bowl, add the onion, garlic, ginger, salt, turmeric and garam masala and mix together.

3. Start adding the gram flour, mixing it into the courgette mixture with your hand. The gram flour is used here to bind the ingredients together into a thick, malleable mixture. (You may need slightly more or less flour, depending on how much moisture there is still in the courgette).

4. Using your hands, shape the mixture into ping pong shaped balls (if baking) or flattened patties (if frying).

5. To cook in a pan: shallow fry the patties for 3-4 minutes each side, until brown and crispy on the outside.

6. To cook in the oven: grease a baking tray with a little oil and lay the balls onto the baking tray. Drizzle a little more oil over the balls and then bake in a hot oven 220C/gas 7, for 30 minutes.

CURRY PUFFS

Any amount of leftover Indian food should be saved, as it is so versatile and often the dishes we create with them are even better second time around! Even if you have just a few tablespoons of curry, meat, lentils, vegetables or just sauce, pop it in a box and stick it away in the freezer.

If using fresh curry, the puffs can also be frozen either raw or once baked.

This is a firm picnic, lunchbox and buffet favourite, and the best way of using up leftovers!

Ingredients

1 sheet ready-made puff pastry

500g of leftovers

1 egg, beaten

1 tsp onion seeds

Handful of fresh coriander, finely chopped

Method

1. Preheat the oven to 190C/gas 5.

2. Put the leftover curry and coriander in to a bowl and mix well.

3. If the ingredients are in large pieces, put the mixture into a food processor and pulse two or three times so that it's still fairly coarse.

4. Roll out the puff pastry sheet to about 3 or 4mm thick, keeping it in a rectangle. Cut out 8 squares and put them on a baking tray one by one with a large spoonful of your filling in the middle of each square.

5. Brush around the edges with beaten egg and fold over into a triangle, then brush all over with more egg. Pinch the edges to get a good seal.

6. Sprinkle onion seeds on top of the egg wash.

7. Bake in the oven for 20 minutes or till golden.

Alternatives:
Great fillings include kheema (p. 105), Rafi's chicken curry (p. 93) or spiced mashed potato (p. 156).

TOMATOES ON TOAST

(V) Vegetarian (🌱) Vegan (👥) Serves 4 people

"This is one of my favourite breakfast/brunch meals. It is super quick, tasty and healthy. Using this recipe as a base, you can experiment with a whole host of different spices. The simplicity of the dish really allows you to fully appreciate the flavour of the individual spices – less is more with this one. Depending on who I am cooking for, I will often add either chilli flakes or fresh chilli to give a bit of heat.

Because I enjoy baking bread, I like to use homemade sourdough, a couple of days old and cooked on a griddle pan." – *Ian*

Ingredients

1 tbsp olive oil

½ tsp of panch pooran (*p. 23*)

6 fresh curry leaves, finely sliced

1-2 cloves of garlic, finely sliced

6 tomatoes, cut into chunks

Squeeze of lemon

Sea salt flakes

4 thick slices of toast

Fresh coriander to garnish

Method

1. Heat the oil in a large frying pan, and when hot add the curry leaves and panch pooran and fry for 1 minute.

2. Add the garlic and continue frying until the garlic just starts to go golden around the edge.

3. Add the tomatoes (the moisture should stop the garlic going from golden to burnt!) and mix well. Fry for 2-3 minutes.

4. Squeeze in a little lemon juice and season well with salt.

5. To serve, squash the tomatoes on top of your toast and garnish with the coriander.

KATI ROLLS

V Vegetarian 👥 Serves 6 people

"This recipe was inspired by the vibrant street food of Kolkata. They're great fun to make, with an omelette layer which sticks to the bread. Get a couple of different salads, fillings and chutneys and let people dive in and build their own personalised wraps. My favourite combination is beef fry *(p. 90)*, red cabbage slaw *(p. 148)* chilli sambal *(p. 24)*, some yoghurt and some coriander chutney *(p. 31)*." – *Ian*

Ingredients

1 tsp vegetable oil

4 eggs

Salt and pepper, to taste

¼ tsp ground cumin

6 cooked chapatis or plain parathas *(p. 20)*

Your choice of filling

Method

1. Prepare whatever main filling and garnishes you would like to use.
2. Beat together the eggs in a bowl along with a pinch of salt and pepper and the ground cumin.
3. Heat a small frying pan with a drizzle of oil. (It is easiest if the pan is around the same size as the breads you are using).
4. When nice and hot, add a couple of large spoonfuls of the egg into the pan. Quickly move it around with a spatula so it covers an area about the same size as your breads.
5. Leave to cook for about 30 seconds, until the egg is starting to set on the bottom, but is still nice and soft and uncooked on the top.
6. Put your bread directly on top of the egg and gently press with a spatula so the bread and egg stick together.
7. Leave for another 20–30 seconds and then flip the whole thing over and cook the other side of the bread for 30 seconds.
8. When ready remove from the pan, so that it is egg side up. Add your desired filling and garnishes, roll up and scoff away!
9. These can be cooked to order or, when the bread and egg are cooked, they can be stacked up and covered with foil until needed.

Alternatives:
There are endless possibilities for fillings for these rolls! Some of our other favourites include: paneer tikka (p. 76), prawn kebabs (p. 109), carrot salad (p. 132) and chutney chicken (p. 94).

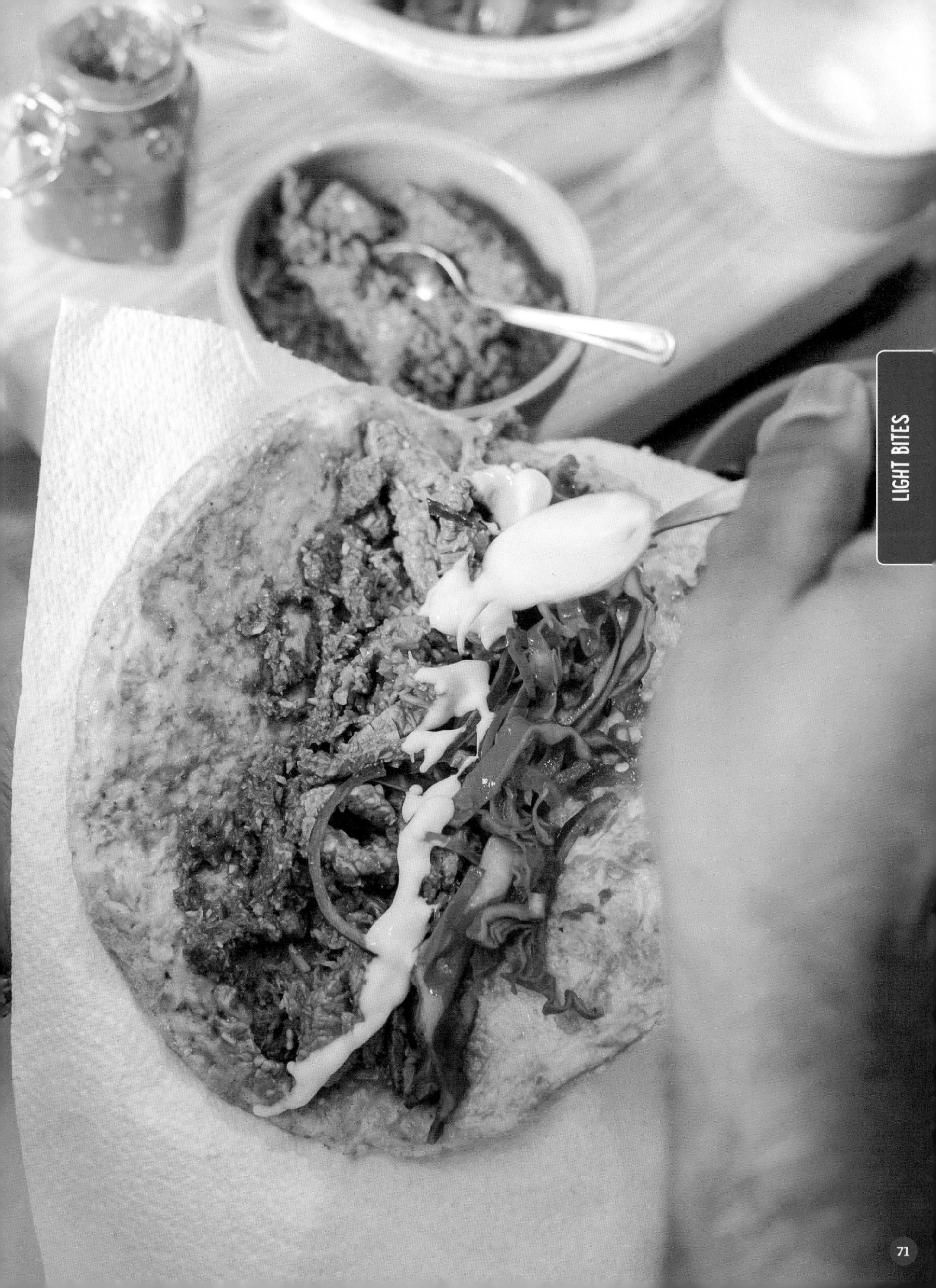

MASALA OMELETTE

(V) Vegetarian (※) Gluten free (👥) Serves 4 people

"This was one our Dad's favourites for breakfast on a Sunday – we have modified his recipe as his version would usually have up to eight green chillies in! We think he made it really hot so he didn't have to share it with us!" – *Lee*

Ingredients

6 eggs

2 tbsp vegetable oil

½ tsp cumin seeds

1 onion, chopped

2 green chillies, thinly sliced

2 tomatoes, chopped

¼ tsp turmeric

½ tsp garam masala

Small handful of fresh coriander

Pinch of salt, to taste

Method

1. Crack the eggs in to a bowl and whisk together with a fork.

2. Heat the oil in a large frying pan. When hot, add the cumin seeds and fry for 1-2 minutes.

3. Add the onion and chilli and fry for 4-5 minutes until the onion has softened.

4. Next, add the tomatoes, turmeric and garam masala, and fry for a further 2 minutes.

5. Add the eggs, coriander, and a pinch of salt. Mix everything and leave to cook for 4-5 minutes until the eggs are set, but still soft.

6. Turn it out and serve with crusty bread and some chilli sauce.

Alternatives:

This dish is so adaptable, depending on what you fancy. You could leave out the tomato, add more onion, add garlic and so on. Try changing the cumin for a different spice: this one change can make a massive difference to the taste of the finished dish, and really lets you appreciate the flavour of the spice. The more savoury, earthy spices work well for this. Try it with a pinch of ajwain seeds, mustard seeds or onion seeds.

MASALA PAPADS

This light snack can also be served on little papads as a canapé before a dinner party.

Using freshly cooked papads is best. The un-popped versions are really easy to cook – either in the microwave, under the grill or even directly on the gas hob!

Ingredients

1 red onion, finely chopped

2 tomatoes, finely chopped

1 tbsp fresh coriander, finely chopped

1 tsp ground cumin

2 tsp amchur powder (mango powder)

Pinch of salt

6 papads (papadums)

Method

1. Mix everything - apart from the papads - together in a bowl and leave to rest for about 30 minutes.

2. Cook the papads, either in the microwave or in some oil in a frying pan.

3. Break the papads in to large pieces and sprinkle the prepared mixture over them just before serving. Or simply serve the mixture in a bowl and let everyone dig in!

PANEER TIKKA KEBABS

(V) Vegetarian (※) Gluten free (👥) Serves 4 people

These simple skewers are just as easy to do under the grill as they are on the barbecue, and everyone loves them! Slightly spiced, with soft centres and crisp corners, they are very comforting. Paneer kebabs served with a salad or two makes for the perfect summer evening meal.

Ingredients

250g paneer, cut into 2cm cubes

2 peppers, cut into large chunks

1 medium onion, cut into large chunks

200g yoghurt

1 inch ginger, finely grated

2 cloves garlic, finely grated

1 tsp ajwain seeds

½ tsp garam masala

1 tsp amchur powder (mango powder)

1 tsp chaat masala powder (p. 55)

1 tsp Kashmiri chilli powder

1 tsp turmeric

1 tsp coriander powder

1 tsp cumin powder

Juice of 1 lemon

Bamboo skewers, soaked in warm water to prevent burning

Vegetable oil for brushing

Method

1. Cut the paneer, peppers and onions into similar-sized chunks and keep to one side.

2. Combine all the remaining ingredients except the oil in a large bowl and whisk together until well mixed. Add the paneer, peppers and onion and mix well.

3. Leave to marinate for at least 2 hours or overnight if possible.

4. Skewer the paneer, peppers and onion alternately onto bamboo skewers. Brush lightly with vegetable oil.

5. These can then be placed on a tray and baked in a hot oven for 15-20 minutes, or under a hot grill for 10 minutes turning occasionally. For best results cook on a barbecue for 3-4 minutes on each side until charred and cooked through.

Top Tip:
We use Kashmiri chilli powder as it's not very hot and gives a nice rounded flavour. If you like it spicy, simply use a hotter chilli powder!

RASAM
(Tomato and Lentil Soup)

 Ⓥ Vegetarian 🌱 Vegan 🌾 Gluten free 👥 Serves 6 people

This recipe is based on the traditional South Indian dish, but is a slightly heartier version with tomato and lentils. The soup is traditionally used to aid digestion and served at the end of a meal with a ball of boiled rice.

Ingredients

For the rasam powder:

1 tsp cumin seeds

2 tsp black peppercorns

1 tsp coriander seeds

½ tsp fenugreek seeds

For the rasam:

2 tbsp vegetable oil

½ tsp mustard oil

2 dry red chillies

6-8 fresh curry leaves

¼ tsp asafoetida

4 cloves of garlic, crushed

½ tsp turmeric

500g passata

900ml water

50g masoor dhal (red lentils)

3 tbsp tamarind paste

Juice of ½ a lemon

Salt, to taste

Method

1. Heat a small frying pan and toast all the spices for the rasam powder for 1-2 minutes. Remove the spices and leave to cool before grinding with a pestle and mortar.

2. Heat the oil in a saucepan over a high heat. Add the mustard seeds and dry chillies and cook for 1-2 minutes until the mustard seeds start to splutter and the chillies begin to darken.

3. Add the asafoetida and curry leaves and cook for a further 30 seconds.

4. Turn the heat down and add the garlic, turmeric and ground rasam powder. Cook for 30 seconds, stirring everything together.

5. Add the passata, water and lentils. Mix well, cover with a lid and simmer for 15-20 minutes, or until the lentils are cooked.

6. Stir in the tamarind paste, lemon juice and add salt to taste. Cook for another 2-3 minutes..

7. Serve with a lump of rice if you wish for a more filling meal.

Top Tip:
If you can't find tamarind, try substituting with more lemon juice.

SPICED SQUASH SOUP

(V) Vegetarian (🌱) Vegan (🌾) Gluten free (👥) Serves 4 people

This is not a traditional Indian dish, but it uses spices to make the most of brilliant seasonal ingredients. It makes a very comforting dish which can be enjoyed on its own, served with toast or naan bread.

Ingredients

1 large butternut squash (or other seasonal squash), cut into chunks

2 onions, cut into chunks

2 tbsp vegetable oil

2 tsp garam masala

1 tsp ground cumin

1 tsp ground coriander

½ tsp turmeric

Pinch of chilli flakes (optional)

700ml vegetable stock

Juice of half a lemon

Salt, to taste

Tarka fry:

2 tbsp vegetable oil

2 cloves of garlic, finely sliced

10 fresh curry leaves, finely sliced

½ tsp onion seeds

2 tbsp desiccated coconut

To garnish: desiccated coconut, toasted in a pan until golden

Method

1. In a large baking tray mix the squash, onion, oil, garam masala, ground cumin, ground coriander, turmeric and chilli flakes. Roast in the oven 200C/gas 6 for 30-40 minutes until the squash is soft.

2. Combine the roasted squash with the vegetable stock and blend until smooth. Add the lemon juice. Transfer to a saucepan and keep warm.

3. In a small frying pan, heat the oil and then fry the curry leaves, onion seeds and garlic for 1-2 minutes.

4. Add the desiccated coconut and fry for 30 seconds, until the coconut has browned. Pour this in to the soup and stir through.

5. Serve sprinkled with more toasted coconut.

Top Tip:
Most butternut squashes have quite a thin skin, so you can leave this on when roasting, but if the squash has a thick skin, it can be removed.

VADA PAV
(Mashed Potato Burger)

 (V) Vegetarian (🌱) Vegan (👥) Serves 6 people

This snack is very famous in Mumbai, and now across the whole of India. There is even a fast food outlet that specialises in just vada pavs.

The vada pav was invented in 1966 by Ashok Vaidy outside Dadar Train Station in Mumbai and is still sold from the same food stall in the same spot by his son, Narendra. This street food is designed as a treat to be eaten on your commute home from work but we love it for lunch (with ketchup)!

Ingredients

1 quantity of spiced mashed potato (*p. 156*)

Batter:

1 Rafi's Spicebox Bhajia pack and salt to taste

Or:

100g gram flour

¼ tsp turmeric

¼ tsp baking powder

¼ tsp chilli powder (or to taste)

Salt to taste

125-150 ml water

Chutneys:

Coriander chutney (*p. 31*)

Coconut chutney (*p. 27*)

Chilli Sambal (*p. 24*)

Other Ingredients:

Soft white bread rolls

Oil for deep frying

Method

1. Mix the batter ingredients together.

2. Form the cold mash potato into round golf ball sized balls (12-15).

3. Coat each mashed potato ball in batter.

4. Deep fry in batches in hot oil for 1-2 minutes, until the potato balls are golden brown all over.

5. To serve, split the bread rolls in half (toast them if you want a crunchier texture) and fill with chutneys and the vada (potato ball). Squish it closed and enjoy!

THE SPICEBOX

A spice box or 'masala (mixture of spices) dabba (box)' is an integral part of our kitchen, and of course our business' namesake!

They are used all over India and by far the easiest way to store your spices. Some like our Grandma's has been passed down a couple of generations and seen a serious amount of action. Once you have one you will never let it go.

Spices are so much happier being kept in the dark and airtight, which makes these tins ideal. Always buy small quantities of the best quality spices you can, so they keep their amazing colour, aroma and flavour. Forget what the supermarkets say they are at their best for 3 to 4 months maximum.

With all your spices in one place you will never go hunting in the back of the cupboards again!

Everyone has their own personal collection of spices within these tins, each one has seven cups and an inner lid where the large bits like cinnamon can be kept. Once you get going you will see that you use some spices a lot more often than others, so you can tailor it to suit your cooking style.

To give you an idea this is the one we use, inside it are some of our favourite things. It gives plenty of scope and is a great place to start.

CUMIN SEEDS

CINNAMON

DRY CHILLIES

GREEN
CARDAMOM

AJWAIN

TURMERIC

ONION
SEEDS

CORIANDER
SEEDS

MUSTARD
SEEDS

STAR ANISE

MEAT & FISH

MEAT & FISH

These dishes can easily be slotted into any type of meal. Add something simple from the veg section and you'll have a perfectly balanced meal. Many of these are absolutely perfect for a barbecue and they can often be prepared ahead, so they're great for a busy lifestyle! ∎

BAKeD STUFFED FISH

This is a Parsi version of a very traditional meal, although every community has its own method. In India this would be wrapped in banana leaves rather than tin foil, but foil works just as well at keeping in all the lovely flavours. Serve with Roasted Cauliflower *(p. 151)* and Lee's Dhal *(p. 144)*.

Ingredients

2 whole sea-bream, gutted and cleaned

2 tsp salt

Juice of 1 lemon

1 quantity of coriander chutney *(p. 31)* or 1 packet of Rafi's Mint and Coriander Raita, defrosted

4 cloves of garlic, peeled and sliced in half lengthways

1 lemon, sliced into rounds

Method

1. Make two deep cuts on either side of the fish and pat with kitchen roll to make sure it is completely dry.

2. Rub the fish all over with the salt and lemon juice, and allow to stand for half an hour.

3. Dry the fish again, removing any liquid and salt. Lay the fish on tin foil, ready to wrap up after stuffing.

4. Stuff the cavity and cuts with the green chutney. Add the garlic cloves and some of the sliced lemon into the cavity, and spread the remaining chutney over the rest of the fish. Add the lemon slices on top.

5. Wrap the fish tightly in the tin foil to make parcels.

6. Bake in the oven at 200C/gas 6 for 30 minutes or until just cooked through.

MEAT & FISH

Alternatives:
Lemon or dover sole.

89

BEEF FRY

This recipe was originally created as a filling for the kati rolls *(p. 71)*, but it's so good it deserves a recipe page all by itself! It's lovely with plain rice, steamed green vegetables and a dollop of chilli sambal *(p. 24)*.

Ingredients

2 tbsp of coconut oil
(or vegetable oil)

10 fresh curry leaves,
finely sliced

2 star anise

1 onion, finely chopped

4-5 cloves of garlic

5cm piece of ginger

1 tsp of ground coriander

1 tsp of ground cumin

½ tsp turmeric

1 tsp ground black
peppercorns

1 tsp of chilli powder

1 tsp of Chinese five spice
(or garam masala)

400g of beef strips

2 tsp of white wine vinegar

20g of desiccated coconut

Salt, to taste

Method

1. Heat the coconut oil in a frying pan and then fry the curry leaves and star anise for 2-3 minutes.

2. Add the onions and continue frying for 5-6 minutes, until they are soft.

3. Using a pestle and mortar or small blender, blitz the garlic and ginger with a little water to form a paste.

4. Add the ginger and garlic paste to the pan and fry for 2 minutes.

5. Add all the spices and fry for another 1-2 minutes. If the spices start to catch on the bottom of the pan add a splash of water to stop them burning.

6. Add the beef and stir fry for 4-5 minutes until cooked to your liking.

7. 1 minute before the end of cooking add the vinegar and coconut.

8. Season with salt, to taste.

RAFI'S CHICKEN CURRY

 Serves 4-6 people

Lee and Kevin grew up eating variations of this dish and they still have very fond memories of it. Rafi would use a whole chicken including bones and skin, and everyone would fight over who got the legs and thighs which have the best flavour and texture.

Ingredients

4 tbsp vegetable oil

4 cloves

6 green cardamoms

2 inch piece cinnamon bark

3 whole star anise

8 fresh curry leaves

1 large onion, finely chopped

2 inch piece fresh ginger, finely chopped

4 cloves garlic, finely chopped

4 tbsp mild curry paste (we use *Fern's curry paste*)

1 tsp turmeric

1 tsp Chinese five spice powder

1.3kg whole chicken, jointed, skinned if preferred

400g chopped tomatoes

115g creamed coconut

½ tsp sugar

Coriander leaves, chopped, to garnish

Salt to taste

Method

1. Heat the oil in a large pan and fry the cloves, cardamoms, cinnamon, star anise and curry leaves until the cloves swell and the curry leaves are dark.

2. Add the onion, ginger and garlic and fry until the onion turns golden brown.

3. Add the paste, turmeric and five spice powder and fry for a few minutes. Add a splash of water and continue to fry until the oil separates.

4. Add the chicken and mix well. When all the chicken is lightly coloured and the spices well distributed, cover and cook gently until the meat is nearly done, stirring occasionally.

5. Add the chopped tomatoes and creamed coconut and simmer gently until the coconut dissolves. The sauce should have a thin consistency at this stage. If not add a splash of water and simmer covered for 5-10 minutes.

6. Season with salt and sugar and add coriander leaves to garnish.

Serving Suggestions

We like to serve this with plain rice, a dhal and a simple salad of cucumber, tomato, onion and fresh chilli.

Top Tip:

Rafi would cook this a day before serving, allowing it to develop in flavour. Leftovers (if any) are perfect served with a fried egg for breakfast the next morning.

CHUTNEY CHICKEN

(V) Gluten free (👥) Serves 4 people

This recipe is so wonderfully simple and the results are fantastic. When we did this for our summer barbecue, the kids just couldn't get enough of them! They're also great for picnics or when watching the football.

Ingredients

3 tbsp of your favourite chutney (we like to use *Geeta's* Lime and Chilli, Mango or Tamarind)

3 tbsp natural yoghurt

500g chicken drumsticks

Method

1. Mix the yoghurt and chutneys together, chopping up any larger pieces in the chutneys if you want a smoother marinade.

2. Score the chicken legs two or three times.

3. Cover the chicken legs in the marinade and leave in the fridge for at least an hour.

4. For best results, barbecue, or cook in the oven at 190C/gas 5 for 45-50 minutes.

Top Tip:
If you would like it a little hotter, stir some chilli powder into the marinade.

SOUTH INDIAN FISH FRY

Gluten free · Serves 4 people

This is a typical dish from the South Indian coastline. You can alter the amount of chilli powder; but the flavour and warmth you get is a real part of this dish. A lovely meal when served with a salad.

Ingredients

4 cloves of garlic, minced

½ tsp turmeric,

1 tsp chilli powder

½ tsp ground black pepper

½ tsp garam masala

Pinch of salt

¼ of a lemon

2 whole mackerel, gutted and cleaned

2 tbsp coconut oil (or vegetable oil)

15-20 fresh curry leaves

Lemon wedges, to serve

Method

1. Combine the minced garlic, turmeric, chilli powder, ground black pepper, garam masala and salt. Squeeze in the lemon juice to create quite a thick paste (depending on the size of the lemon, you might need a little more or little less).

2. Make three deep cuts into each side of the fish.

3. Spread the paste evenly all over the fish and inside the cuts. Leave these to marinate for 30 mins.

4. Heat the coconut oil in a large frying pan. When nice and hot, add the fish.

5. Try not to move the fish, so it crisps up. After 2-3 minutes, turn the fish over and add the curry leaves, in the oil around the fish. Fry for a further 2-3 minutes, until cooked.

6. Remove from the pan and serve with the lemon wedges to squeeze over the fish.

MEAT & FISH

Top Tip:
Lots of other fish can be used, such as whole sea bass or fish steaks like salmon. Depending on the thickness of the fish (and how you like it), it might need a little longer in the pan.

SPICED FISHCAKES

 Serves 4 people

"This recipe is inspired by our Aunty Jane. A version of these fishcakes would always be on the table when we went to visit and more often than not she would bring a batch with her if she came to visit. A perfect little snack and a great addition to any party spread." – *Kevin*

Ingredients

450g firm white fish such as haddock, coley or cod, skinned

2 medium potatoes, boiled and mashed

4 spring onions, finely chopped

2 green chillies, finely chopped

1 inch ginger, finely grated

Small handful coriander leaves finely chopped

2 tbsp coriander seeds, roasted and coarsely crushed

Salt and pepper to taste

2 eggs, beaten

Flour for dusting

Breadcrumbs to coat

Oil for frying

Method

1. Steam the fish until just cooked, cool and break up into small flakes removing any bones.

2. Dry roast the coriander seeds and coarsely crush in a pestle and mortar or coffee grinder and set aside.

3. When the fish is cool combine with the potato, coriander seeds, spring onions, chilli, ginger, coriander leaves, salt and one egg. Mix well until the mixture is well incorporated. Place in the fridge for 30 minutes to cool and firm up.

4. Shape the mixture into small round flat cakes, dip into flour then egg then breadcrumbs.

5. Either shallow fry in small batches turning once or alternatively deep-fry until evenly golden all over.

6. Best served warm with a chilli sauce or raita style dip.

Top Tip:
These are perfect served with the crushed peas (p. 159) as a starter or light lunch.

Once cooked, these freeze really well. Simply defrost and re-heat in the oven.

GOAN PORK PICKLE

Gluten free · Makes several jars

This unusual meat pickle is inspired by Rafi's much loved pheasant pickle. The flavours are intense and it is best served as a condiment alongside other dishes.

This will keep in the fridge for up to 4 weeks and makes a perfect foodie gift!

Ingredients

6 dried red chillies

175ml cider vinegar

2 tsp cumin seeds

1 tsp fennel seeds

25 black peppercorns

6 cloves of garlic

20g fresh ginger, peeled

½ tsp turmeric

2 tsp garam masala

2 tsp of salt

2 tsp sugar

800g boneless belly pork, skin removed, cut in to roughly 2cm cubes.

4 tbsp vegetable oil

Method

1. Break the dried chillies into a few pieces and add to the vinegar. Leave to soak for an hour.

2. In a hot, dry pan toast the cumin seeds, fennel seeds and peppercorns for 1-2 minutes, until the cumin has browned and smells nutty.

3. Allow the spices to cool a little and then grind to a fine powder.

4. Add the ground spices, garlic, ginger, turmeric, garam masala, salt and sugar to the vinegar.

5. Using a blender (or stick blender) purée the spicy vinegar mix. Add this to the pieces of pork and mix everything together. Cover and leave to marinate in the fridge for 24 hours.

6. The next day, heat the oil in a large pan. Add the pork with all of the marinade and mix well. Cover with a lid and cook on the hob on a low heat for around 1 hour until the meat is very tender.

7. Squish the meat with a wooden spoon so that it breaks apart into a coarse texture.

8. Turn up the heat and cook for another 5-6 minutes, until reduced slightly and thickened.

9. Leave to cool. It can be eaten immediately, at room temperature, or bottled in sterilised jars and kept in the fridge.

MEAT & FISH

GRILLED LAMB CHOPS

 Gluten free Serves 4 people

Perfect for a party and are always a big hit at our annual staff summer barbecue.

Ingredients

Handful of mint leaves, approximately 20

1 inch fresh ginger

1 inch piece cinnamon bark

1 tsp coriander seeds

½ tsp salt

1 tsp fennel seeds

½ tsp chilli powder

1 tsp garam masala

1 tsp turmeric

1 tbsp vegetable oil

1 tbsp water

8 lamb chops

2 tbsp lemon juice

Method

1. Using a coffee grinder, blitz together the first 11 ingredients, to form a smooth paste.

2. Spread this marinade over both sides of the lamb and leave in the fridge to marinate for at least 2 hours.

3. Just before cooking pour over the lemon juice, and leave for 5 minutes.

4. Cook under a hot grill for 4-5 minutes on each side until cooked to your liking and charred on the outside.

Top Tip:
These chops are great served with a fresh coriander chutney (p. 31) and green salad.

RAFI'S KHEEMA
(Mince Curry)

Serves 4 people

"One of our family favourites, my mum would always serve this dish with chapatis, a simple dhal and a light salad. I love it for breakfast on toast, with a fried egg!" – *Kevin*

Ingredients

1 tbsp vegetable oil

1 large onion, finely chopped

½ tsp onion seeds

½ tsp mustard seeds

2 dry red chillies

8 fresh curry leaves

2 cloves garlic, crushed

2 inch ginger, finely grated

4 green chillies, finely chopped (de-seeded if preferred)

2 tbsp of mild curry paste (we like *Fern's curry paste*)

450g lean minced beef or lamb

250g passata or chopped tomatoes

225g frozen peas

Large handful coriander leaves, chopped

Salt to taste

Method

1. Heat the oil in a large saucepan and fry the onions, seeds, dry chillies and curry leaves until the onion is translucent.

2. Stir in the ginger, garlic, green chilli and curry paste and fry for a further 5 minutes.

3. Add 300ml water and reduce until the oil separates and a paste forms.

4. Add the mince and stir well using the back of the spoon to break up the mince as much as possible. Add the tomatoes or passata and cook gently with a lid on for a further 20 minutes.

5. Once the mince is cooked, add the peas and cook for a further 5 minutes. Garnish with coriander and season well.

Top Tip:

Kheema makes great leftovers. It can be turned into fillings for samosas or curry puffs (p. 67), or even a spicy shepherd's pie using our Spiced Mash recipe (p. 156)!

KOFTA (Spiced meatballs)

Gluten free · Makes roughly 14 · Serves 4 people

These meatballs are great served in a wrap with carrot salad *(p. 132)* or a drizzle of yoghurt, pomegranate seeds and some fresh mint. They also go deliciously in a curry, try adding them to the egg curry sauce *(p. 127)*.

Ingredients

500g of minced beef or lamb

2 cloves of garlic, finely grated

2 cm piece of ginger, finely grated

2 green chillies, very finely sliced

1 onion, finely chopped

A handful of fresh coriander, chopped

1 egg

1 potato (about 100g), grated

½ tsp turmeric

2 tsp garam masala

Pinch of salt

Method

1. Add all of the ingredients to a mixing bowl. Using your hands, squish everything together for 2-3 minutes, until fully combined.

2. Shape the mixture into balls (about the size of golf balls), put them on a plate and leave them to rest in the fridge for 30 minutes.

3. The koftas can then be cooked by shallow frying, for 10-15 minutes or roasted in the oven, with a drizzle of oil, for about 25 minutes, at gas mark 220C/gas 7.

Alternatives:
These would be perfect to serve in Rafi's Pasanda Curry pack.

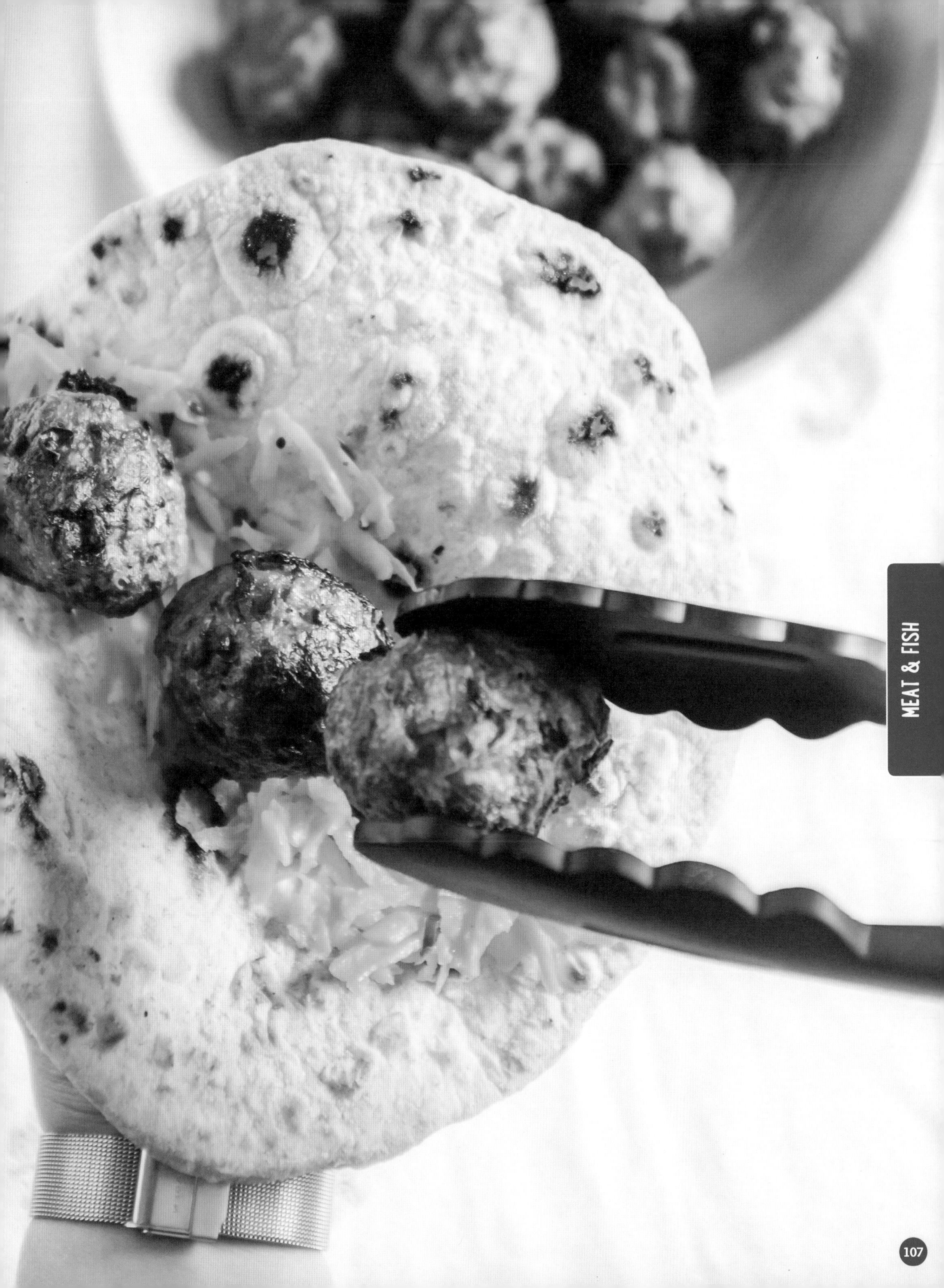

PRAWN KEBABS

Gluten free   Serves 4 people

These kebabs are a typical street food from Goa and Kerala - the sort of snack you might come across while walking along a beach. We love cooking these up on the barbecue as they always go down a treat.

Ingredients

1 tsp cardamom seeds

2 tsp cumin seeds

2 tsp coriander seeds

½ tsp ground cinnamon

1 tsp turmeric

1 garlic clove, finely grated or crushed

1 tsp paprika

2 tbsp vegetable oil

200g fresh, raw king prawns

Salt to taste

Lime wedges to serve

Bamboo skewers, soaked in warm water to prevent burning

Method

1. Dry roast the cardamom, cumin and coriander seeds in a small frying pan for 2-3 minutes or until golden and aromatic. Leave to cool.

2. Grind the roasted seeds in a pestle and mortar or coffee grinder until fine. Combine with all remaining ingredients in a bowl. Add the prawns and stir well to coat them all. Leave to marinate for at least 1 hour.

3. Just before cooking, season well with salt. Thread 3-4 prawns onto a skewer and continue until all the prawns are used.

4. Cook under a hot grill for 2-3 minutes on each side until cooked and slightly charred. Serve immediately with wedges of lime.

Top Tip:
You can also stir-fry these tasty prawns. Simply cook the marinated prawns in a very hot pan for a few minutes until thoroughly cooked and finish with a squeeze of lime and chopped fresh coriander.

MOGHUL STYLE ROAST LAMB (Shahi Raan)

 Gluten free Serves 8 people

In India this is a celebration dish often enjoyed at weddings. It's a real show stopper but also very easy – great for if you're hosting a dinner party or just want a simple Sunday roast with a twist.

Ingredients

4 onions, chopped

4 cloves of garlic

2 inch fresh ginger

3 tbsp ground almonds

2 tsp cumin powder

2 tsp coriander powder

2 tsp turmeric

2 tsp garam masala

4-6 green chillies

Juice of one lemon

Salt, to taste

300ml natural yoghurt

1 tsp black cumin

Leg of lamb (about 1.8kg)

Toasted flaked almonds, to garnish (optional)

Method

1. In a food processor blend the first 11 ingredients to make a smooth paste.

2. Gradually add the yoghurt, mixing well.

3. Stir through the black cumin.

4. Make two or three deep diagonal cuts on either side of the thick end of the meat.

5. Put the meat on a baking tray and push some of the spice mixture into the cuts. Spread the remainder all over the meat.

6. Cover the tray loosely with foil and roast for 2-2 ½ hours at 190C/gas 5. Remove the foil for the last 10 minutes of cooking.

7. Allow the meat to rest for 10-15 minutes before carving. Garnish with toasted flaked almonds if you wish.

Alternatives:

The spice mixture is very versatile and you could use it on lamb chops, a beef joint or chicken legs.

We like to serve this dish simply, with tomatoes roasted with chilli flakes and salt (p. 155), a salad, a dhal (p. 144) and chapatis (p. 20).

SEEKH KEBAB
(Minced Meat Kebabs)

Gluten free   Makes 12 small kebabs

We love to simply serve these kebabs in flatbreads with yoghurt and salad. This is a great recipe to cook with children as they can get stuck into mixing and shaping the meat.

Ingredients

4-5 large cloves of garlic

2 inch ginger

500g lamb mince

1 finely chopped onion

2 tsp ground cumin

2 tsp ground coriander

2 tsp garam masala

2-3 tsp Kashmiri chilli powder

2 tsp amchur powder (mango powder)

1 tsp salt

Method

1. Using a pestle and mortar or small blender, blitz the garlic and ginger with a little water to form a paste.

2. In a large bowl add the mince, garlic and ginger paste, all the spices and salt.

3. Get stuck in with your hands, squeezing all the ingredients through your fingers and kneading it together almost like a ball of dough. Do this for 3-4 minutes so that everything is really well combined. This kneading of the meat will also help it stay together when cooking.

4. Take small balls of the mixture and mould it into a sausage shape (you want to try and compress it quite tightly together). Lay them directly on a grill pan, ready for cooking. You should be able to get about 12 small kebabs (or 6 large kebabs) out of the mixture.

5. Cook the kebabs under a hot grill for 15-20 minutes, turning half-way through cooking.

MEAT & FISH

TAMARIND SALMON

🌾 Gluten free 👥 Serves 4 people

"This is my favourite mid-week meal, and it's ready in less than 20 minutes!
I sometimes add a chopped lemongrass stalk to the marinade if I'm feeling
Thai-inspired, and serve it alongside noodles and fried greens." – *Hana*

Ingredients

4 salmon fillets

4 tbsp tamarind chutney
(we like *Geeta's* for this
recipe)

Juice of 2 limes

2 finely sliced red chillies
(de-seeded if you wish)

Handful of chopped fresh
coriander leaves

Method

1. Mix together the chutney, lime juice and chillies.

2. Cover the salmon fillets in the sticky marinade,
   and leave to marinate for 20-30 minutes if
   you have the time.

3. Preheat your oven to 180C/gas 4.

4. Roast the salmon fillets for 15-20 minutes
   or cooked to your liking.

5. Garnish with chopped coriander
   and lime wedges.

Alternatives:
*You can use this
marinade on chicken
or white fish.*

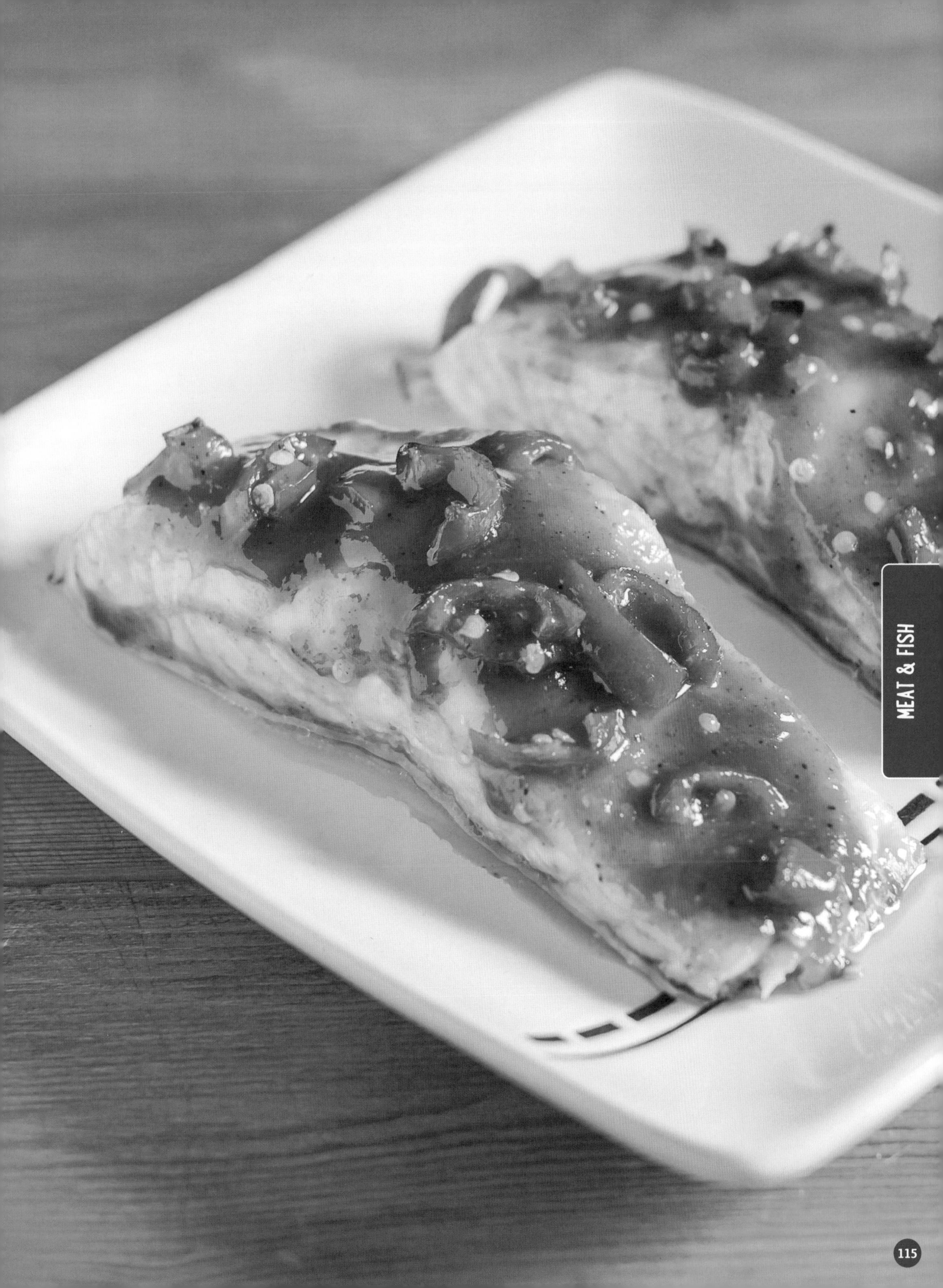

VEG

Vegetables are an essential part of every Indian meal. They add amazing colour, texture and freshness to any menu. We've created some surprising and vibrant dishes which will really showcase our fantastic seasonal produce. ∎

VEG

117

IAN'S AUBERGINE AND COCONUT FRY

(V) Vegetarian Vegan Gluten free Serves 4 people

"This is one of my favourite ways to cook aubergine. Don't be afraid of getting the pan nice and hot and charring the aubergines so they are quite dark. This gives the dish a deep, savoury flavour as well as providing contrasting textures.

Sometimes I like to leave it to cool and then smush it together with a drizzle of olive oil and a squeeze of lemon to make a dip for bread." – *Ian*

Ingredients

3-4 tbsp of vegetable oil

½ tsp of mustard seeds

6-8 fresh curry leaves, sliced

1 large aubergine, cut into small chunks

1 clove of garlic, finely sliced

¼ tsp turmeric

10g desiccated coconut

Salt to taste

Method

1. Heat the oil in a large frying pan until hot.

2. Add the mustard seeds and fry them until they start to pop.

3. Add the curry leaves, let them sizzle briefly and then add the aubergine.

4. Fry for 6-8 minutes until the aubergine is soft all the way through and charred on the outside.

5. Lower the temperature and add the garlic and turmeric. Cook for 1-2 minutes, adding a splash of water to stop them from burning.

6. Add the coconut and fry for a further 2 minutes to coat the aubergine and brown the coconut.

7. Season well with salt and serve.

VEG

AVIYAL
(Coconut and Yoghurt Broth)

 (V) Vegetarian (※) Gluten free (👥) Serves 4 people

This is a lovely, light, South Indian dish which is cooked in an unusual way. It makes a great accompaniment to richer curries.

Aviyal is prepared in many South Indian temples for mass lunches. The vegetables traditionally used are gourds, aubergine, beans, drumsticks, cucumber, potato, carrots and peas, but you can use whatever is in season and looks tasty!

Ingredients

4 tbsp desiccated coconut

2 cloves garlic

1 green chilli

1 tsp cumin seeds

Salt to taste

250ml water

450g mixed vegetables, cut into bite-size pieces

150ml natural yoghurt

½ tsp cornflour, whisked into the yoghurt (this will reduce the likelihood of the yoghurt splitting)

3-4 fresh curry leaves

3 tbsp coconut oil (optional)

Method

1. Grind together the coconut, garlic, chilli, cumin and salt.

2. Bring the water to the boil in a large pan and simmer the vegetables until half cooked.

3. Reduce the heat and add the ground coconut mixture, yoghurt and curry leaves to the water.

4. Continue to simmer gently until the vegetables are cooked. Season with salt to taste.

5. For a traditional finish, add the coconut oil and stir through before removing from the heat to enhance the flavour.

BEETROOT CURRY

"I had this dish a number of times in Sri Lanka. It's amazing to look at and always surprises guests as beetroot is not an ingredient you will find in many Indian restaurants in the UK." – *Kevin*

Ingredients

2 tbsp vegetable oil

1 tsp cumin seeds

1 tsp mustard seeds

2 cloves garlic, sliced

1 dry red chilli

8 fresh curry leaves

1 tsp turmeric

300g raw beetroot, peeled and cubed into 2cm cubes

1 tin coconut milk

Juice of half a lemon

Salt

Method

1. Heat the oil in a deep saucepan or small wok. Add the mustard, cumin seeds, chilli and curry leaves and fry for 5 minutes until chilli turns dark.

2. Add the garlic and fry gently for 2-3 minutes.

3. Add the beetroot and turmeric and mix well and cook for 5 minutes.

4. Add the coconut milk and cook on a gentle simmer without a lid to reduce down to a rich sauce. The beetroot should be firm but cooked through. If the sauce thickens too quickly, simply add water and reduce further until the beetroot is fully cooked.

5. Once cooked, add salt and lemon juice and serve hot.

Top Tip:

This is a rich, thick dish. We like to serve it with light dishes like Broccoli Upkari (p. 163) and Kachoombar (p. 139).

VEG

COURGETTE CURRY

(V) Vegetarian (👽) Vegan (🌾) Gluten free (👥) Serves 4 people

This is the perfect recipe when the garden or the allotment is completely overrun with courgettes! Vegetables always taste delicious in season, and the flavours of the courgettes really shine through in this simple sauce.

We use garam masala at the very end of this recipe. It has a warming, toasted flavour which enhances this simple dish.

Ingredients

2 tbsp vegetable oil

½ tsp cumin seeds

½ tsp mustard seeds

1 onion, diced

2 cloves garlic, sliced

¼ tsp ground turmeric

¼ tsp chilli powder

2 tsp cumin and coriander powder

675g courgettes (5 courgettes), sliced into rounds

1 tbsp tomato purée

1 tin chopped tomatoes

150ml water

2 tsp garam masala

Salt to taste

1 tbsp chopped fresh coriander

Method

1. Heat the oil in a pan and add the cumin and mustard seeds until they splutter.

2. Turn the heat down, add onion and garlic and fry for 5-7 minutes until the onions are translucent.

3. Add turmeric, chilli powder, coriander, cumin and courgettes and keep stirring. Fry for a further 5 minutes.

4. Add the tomato purée, the tinned tomatoes and water. Stir, cover and simmer for 10 minutes.

5. When nearly ready to serve, stir in the garam masala, salt and simmer for 5 minutes until thickened to your liking.

6. Garnish with chopped coriander leaves.

Alternatives:

Courgettes can be substituted for marrows, or any abundant vegetables, if you've taken your eye off your veg plot!

RAFI'S BOILED EGG CURRY

(V) Vegetarian (🌾) Gluten free (👥) Serves 4 people

This is another famous dish from Rafi's collection. She would always serve this as it is, with a vegetable pilau *(p. 51)*.

"Lee and I would love to eat the eggs with the yolk removed and the cavity filled with yogurt – the trick is to try to get the whole thing in your mouth at once! Not that easy when you're five years old!" – *Kevin*

Ingredients

2 tsp white poppy seeds

2 tsp sesame seeds

2 tsp coriander seeds

2 tbsp desiccated coconut

350ml tomato juice

2 tsp gram flour

1 tsp chilli powder

¼ tsp asafoetida

Salt to taste

1 tsp sugar

6 hard-boiled eggs, halved

2 tbsp sesame oil

1 tsp cumin seeds

4 whole dry chillies

8 fresh curry leaves

4 cloves garlic, finely sliced

Method

1. Toast the poppy, sesame and coriander seeds in a dry small frying pan for 3-4 minutes.

2. Add the coconut and toast it until it browns. Remove from the heat and transfer to a plate or bowl to stop cooking and allow to cool.

3. Grind the toasted ingredients together in a pestle and mortar or coffee grinder.

4. Add the toasted ingredients, gram flour, chilli powder, asafoetida, salt and sugar to the tomato juice and whisk well to combine.

5. Transfer to a saucepan and bring to the boil.

6. Reduce the heat and simmer gently for 10-15 minutes.

7. While the sauce is reducing, heat the oil in a small frying pan, add remaining ingredients, except the eggs and fry until the chilli and garlic turn brown.

8. Pour the hot spices and oil over the curry sauce.

9. Add the hard-boiled eggs and shake the pan gently to cover the eggs with the sauce.

10. Simmer for a further 3-4 minutes. Serve hot.

Alternatives:
This sauce is really unique. It has a great savoury flavour and smooth consistency so it is perfect for any vegetables. Try it with roasted diced aubergine or boiled new potatoes and peas.

VEG

BRUSSEL SPROUTS AND AJWAIN

(V) Vegetarian Vegan Gluten free Serves 4 people

This is another incredibly simple side dish which is brilliant to have up your sleeve when you need to include some vegetables.

"Like many people I used to HATE sprouts. Then I discovered cooking them this way, and now I can't get enough!" – *Lee*

Ingredients

2 tbsp vegetable oil

½ tsp ajwain seeds, lightly crushed

2 cloves garlic, sliced

300g shredded sprouts (any greens are good – try French beans, kale or spring greens)

½ tsp turmeric

Salt, to taste

Squeeze of lemon

Method

1. Heat the oil in a wok, add the ajwain and garlic and fry over a medium heat for 30-40 seconds.

2. Add the sprouts and turmeric then fry for a further 2-3 minutes.

3. Add 2-3 tsp of water and cook until it evaporates.

4. Season to taste, and garnish with lemon juice.

CABBAGE AND EGG SCRAMBLE

(V) Vegetarian (꽃) Gluten free (👥) Serves 4 people

"This dish is inspired by an egg dish we often had at lunch time when we were staying in a village in the foothills of the Himalayas. When we went walking in the hills, this was our favourite dish to find when we opened up our tiffin tins. We'd eat it at room temperature with lots of homemade aloo parathas (we'd be full after one or two parathas, but our guides would eat at least five!).
Very simple, but very comforting home cooked food." – *Ian*

Ingredients

2 tbsp vegetable oil

½ tsp ajwain seeds

½ tsp crushed fenugreek seeds

Pinch of chilli flakes (optional)

1 large clove of garlic, finely sliced

1 pointed/sweetheart cabbage, finely sliced

½ tsp turmeric

¼ lemon

2 eggs, beaten

1 tsp garam masala

Salt, to taste

Method

1. Heat the oil in a large frying pan and fry the ajwain seeds, fenugreek seeds and chilli flakes for 1 minute.

2. Add the garlic and fry for 1 minute, until it starts to brown around the edges.

3. Add the cabbage and stir fry for 2 minutes.

4. Add the turmeric and a splash of water and continue to cook for 3-4 minutes, until the cabbage is cooked, but still has a little crunch.

5. Squeeze in the lemon juice and mix.

6. Add the eggs and cook for 2-3 minutes, scrambling them in with the cabbage and mixing everything together.

7. Just before serving, sprinkle over the garam masala and add salt to taste.

VEG

CARROT SALAD

 (V) Vegetarian Vegan Gluten free Serves 4 people

Everything tastes better when served with this salad. We serve it at every staff event, and everyone loves the crunch and colour it brings. It's great as a topping for burgers.

Ingredients

350g grated carrot

2 finely sliced green chillies (optional)

1 tbsp olive oil

¼ tsp mustard seeds

¼ tsp cumin seeds

¼ tsp turmeric

¼ tsp salt

¼ tsp sugar

Juice of 1 lemon

Handful of chopped fresh coriander leaves

Method

1. Heat the oil in a small pan over a medium heat and then add the mustard and cumin seeds. Heat gently for 1-2 minutes.

2. Add the turmeric to the pan, turning off the heat. Leave the spices to cool for 5 minutes.

3. Mix the lemon juice, salt and sugar with the carrots and chillies (if using). Pour over the spiced oil and mix well.

4. Cover and leave for 30 minutes.

5. Garnish with coriander leaves just before serving.

Alternatives:
Try using finely sliced vegetables, like fennel or cucumber.

DHAL MAKHANI

Ⓥ Vegetarian   🌾 Gluten free   👥 Serves 4-6 people

"Dhal makhani is a typical Punjabi-style dish and the addition of butter and cream makes it very rich. I had this dish many times whilst touring Rajasthan, it often featured on their famous thalis and goes excellently with naan bread. As a really authentic touch, a lump of hot charcoal is added to the pan with a drop of ghee on it to infuse a deep smoky flavour." — *Kevin*

Ingredients

1 cup black dhal (lentil) (whole urid with skin), soaked overnight

1 tin red kidney beans, drained

25g butter

1 tbsp vegetable oil

1 tsp cumin seeds

1 onion, finely chopped

½ tsp chilli powder

4 cloves garlic, finely chopped

2 inch ginger, grated

2 tbsp tomato purée

1 tsp garam masala

A pinch of kasuri methi (dried fenugreek leaves)

Method

1. Heat the vegetable oil and butter in a large saucepan, add the cumin seeds and fry for 2-3 minutes.

2. Add the onion, garlic, ginger and chilli powder, and fry until the onion is soft.

3. Add the tomato purée and fry for a further 3 minutes.

4. Add the drained lentils and kidney beans and cover with water. Bring to the boil, cover and reduce the heat, and simmer gently for at least 20 minutes or until the lentils are soft.

5. Using a stick blender blitz for 1 minute, retaining some texture. Add hot water if it is too thick - it should have a thick yet pouring consistency.

6. Once the lentils are cooked, add the garam masala and methi leaves and cream. Season and serve hot.

Alternatives:
Add as much cream as desired. Use crème fresh for a lighter finish.

VEG

135

SPICED GREEN BEANS

(V) Vegetarian (🌱) Vegan (🌾) Gluten free (👥) Serves 4 people

Don't be fooled by how ridiculously simple this is, the results will blow you away.

Ingredients

1 tbsp vegetable oil

500g green beans

½ tsp turmeric

½ tsp chilli flakes
(or to taste)

1 tsp salt

Juice of 1 lime

Method

1. Heat the oil in a frying pan and add the beans.

2. Cook for 3 minutes or until tender.

3. Remove from the heat and stir through the turmeric, salt, chilli flakes and the lime juice.

4. Serve hot.

Alternatives:
It will work with just about any beans such as, mange tout, sugar snap peas or finely sliced runner beans.

136

KACHOOMBAR
(Chopped Salad)

(V) Vegetarian   (🌱) Vegan   (🌾) Gluten free   (👥) Serves 4 people

This is a fresh Parsi-style salad, perfect for adding a crunchy, zingy element to your meal. It's usually made with onion, tomato and cucumber, but here we have opted for radishes, onion and sweet pepper.

Ingredients

200g of radishes, finely sliced

1 red pepper, cut into small cubes

1 red onion, finely chopped

1-2 green chillies, finely sliced (optional)

½ tsp ground cumin

Juice and zest of 1 lemon

¼ tsp sugar

½ tsp onion seeds, toasted

Pinch of salt, to taste

A handful of fresh chopped coriander

Method

1. Combine all the ingredients in a bowl.
2. Simply leave to rest in the fridge for 30 mins and serve chilled. Quick, easy and tasty!

VEG

YOGHURT CURRY
(Kadhi)

(V) Vegetarian (※) Gluten free (👥) Serves 4 people

This is a fresh and light dish which is very quick and easy to make. The yoghurt gives this sauce a texture and tangy flavour, very different from a lot of other curries. It is often served as it is, with rice and a simple vegetable dish or try adding courgette koftas *(p. 64)* or bhajias to the sauce.

Ingredients

450g of set yoghurt

300ml water

1 tbsp gram flour

¼ tsp turmeric

Pinch of salt

2 tbsp vegetable oil

1 dry chilli

½ tsp cumin seeds

½ tsp mustard seeds

¼ tsp fenugreek seeds

¼ tsp asafoetida

5-6 fresh curry leaves

2 cloves of garlic, crushed

1 inch ginger, cut into thin matchsticks

Method

1. Add the yoghurt, water, gram flour, turmeric and salt to a sauce pan and whisk together until fully combined and there are no lumps of gram flour.

2. Bring the yoghurt mix to the boil, turn the heat down and simmer for about 10 minutes, stirring it from time to time.

3. Heat the oil in a small frying pan and then fry the dry chilli, mustard seeds, fenugreek seeds asafoetida and curry leaves for 2-3 minutes, until the mustard seeds begin to crackle and the chill starts to turn black.

4. Add in the garlic and ginger and fry for a further 1-2 minutes, until the garlic starts to brown around the edges.

5. Pour the spices into the yoghurt mix and cover with a lid. Turn off the heat and leave to sit for 2 minutes. Before serving stir the spices fully into the yoghurt mix.

POTATOES IN A HOT RED SAUCE (Lal Batata)

V Vegetarian **🌱** Vegan
🌾 Gluten free **👥** Serves 4 people

This recipe is not for the faint-hearted - it has lots of big flavours from the chillies and the tamarind. You can reduce the amount of chillies used, or deseed them before use if you would like less heat.

As usual with spiced recipes, this tastes even better the day after you've made it.

Ingredients

500g new potatoes

1 ½ tsp cumin seeds

½ tsp mustard seeds

25g dried Kashmiri chillies (or standard dried red chillies)

4 cloves garlic

1-2 tbsp vegetable oil

3 tbsp *Geeta's* tamarind chutney OR 4 tbsp tamarind juice plus 10g jaggery *(p. 170)*

2 tbps tomato purée

4 fresh curry leaves

¼ tsp asafoetida

Salt and sugar to taste

Method

1. Boil the potatoes whole (there is no need to peel them).
2. Soak dried chillies in enough just-boiled water to cover. Once plump, drain.
3. Dry fry the cumin and mustard seeds until fragrant.
4. Grind the seeds with the garlic cloves in a pestle and mortar. Add the chillies and the vegetable oil, and grind together to form a paste (you can also use a stick blender). Add the tomato purée, tamarind, curry leaves and asafoetida and mix well.
5. Fry the resulting paste until the oil separates.
6. Add the boiled potatoes and simmer for 5 minutes.
7. Adjust seasoning to taste and serve with chapatis or paratha.

Alternatives:
Other root vegetables would work well with this, such as butternut squash or carrots. Roast aubergines are also lovely in this sauce.

VEG

LEE'S TARKA DHAL

 Vegetarian · Vegan · Gluten free · Serves 4 people

"This is an old family favourite passed down by our grandmother, and my mum and I have since adapted it even further. A version of this should feature in most Indian meals - it is a great accompaniment and also a great source of protein.

We are always amazed how unpopular lentils and dhal are in this country, particularly in mainstream Indian restaurants. Every time we cook it at home for family and friends it tends to be the dish that everyone falls in love with." — *Lee*

Ingredients

130g masoor dhal (red lentils)

50g toor dhal (lentil)

350ml water

3 chillies left whole with stalk removed

1 tsp turmeric

1 small onion, sliced

For the tarka:

4 tbsp vegetable oil

½ tsp cumin seeds

½ tsp mustard seeds

6 fresh curry leaves

2 dried chillies

¼ tsp asafoetida

1 clove garlic, thinly sliced

Salt to taste

Coriander leaves to garnish

Method

1. Place the first 6 ingredients in pan and bring to the boil. Cover and simmer very gently for at least 30 minutes, until the water has evaporated. Try not to peek in the pan as this will lengthen the cooking time.

2. Mash the lentils with the back of a spoon. When smooth, thin the mixture with hot water to achieve a single cream consistency.

3. Now for the tarka - heat the oil in a small frying pan, add in the mustard and cumin seeds, curry leaves, dried chillies and asafoetida and fry until the chillies turn dark and the seeds start to pop. Add in the garlic and cook until golden brown. As soon as it is golden, pour the oil and spices over the lentils and cover.

4. Leave to rest for 5 minutes, mix well, season with salt and garnish with picked coriander leaves.

Top Tips:

You can use any split lentil. Using the red lentils ensures a nice smooth texture while the toor dhal adds a little more bite. Other lentils that work well are chana dhal and moong dhal.

Rafi would add tinned plum tomatoes before the tarka. This will give you a sweeter, rounded finish to the dhal.

OKRA FRY

In our opinion, this is the best way to eat okra. Okra has an unusual flavour, but it looks beautiful when sliced, like little stars. When fried in this way it becomes crisp and you could serve it as a nibble with drinks, or as an accompaniment to your main course.

Ingredients

350g okra

½ tsp salt

½ tsp turmeric

½ tsp chilli powder

3 tbsp vegetable oil

½ tsp mustard seeds

Handful fresh coriander

Method

1. Cut okra into 2.5 cm slices, rub with the turmeric, chilli powder and salt.

2. Heat oil in a pan and add the mustard seeds until they crackle.

3. Add the okra and fry uncovered until they are nice and crisp, stirring occasionally.

4. Serve hot, garnished with fresh coriander.

VEG

LEE'S RED CABBAGE SLAW

 (V) Vegetarian (🌱) Vegan (🌾) Gluten free (👥) Serves 4-6 people

"I first made this at a cafe I used to run and it was very popular. I use to serve it in pitta sandwiches, with spiced potatoes and mixed in salads... well, everywhere really!" — *Lee*

Ingredients

½ red cabbage, finely sliced

2 small red onions, finely sliced

Juice of 2 lemons

2 tsp sugar

2 tbsp olive oil

10 fresh curry leaves

1 tsp cumin seeds

Salt to taste

Method

1. Slice the cabbage and onions as finely as possible.

2. Add the sugar to the lemon juice to dissolve and add to the cabbage and stir well.

3. Heat the oil in a small frying pan. When hot, add the cumin seeds and curry leaves. Fry on a medium heat until the cumin seeds start to crackle. Remove the pan from the heat and leave to cool.

4. Once the oil is cool pour over the cabbage and stir well, season to taste and leave overnight in the fridge to develop flavours.

Top Tip:
Make this the day before if possible, as the lemon juice transforms the colour of the red cabbage into a vibrant pink.

SPICED ROAST CAULIFLOWER

 (V) Vegetarian (🌱) Vegan (🌾) Gluten free (👥) Serves 4 people

Cauliflower has a nice, subtle flavour which acts as a great foil for spices. Roasting it helps bring out the sweetness and when the edges catch it adds a slight bitterness and a different texture.

Ingredients

1 cauliflower, broken in to small florets, and cut so that all are a similar size

3 tbsp vegetable oil

2 tsp ground cumin

2 tsp ground coriander

½ tsp chilli powder

1 tsp turmeric

1 tsp onion seeds

Salt, to taste

Lemon wedges

Method

1. Mix the cauliflower with the oil and all the spices.

2. Lay out on a baking tray and roast in the oven at gas mark 220C/ gas 7 for about 25 minutes, until cooked through and browned.

3. Season to taste with salt and serve with lemon wedge to squeeze over.

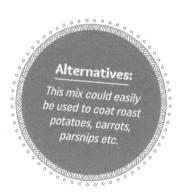

Alternatives:
This mix could easily be used to coat roast potatoes, carrots, parsnips etc.

VEG

151

ROAST SQUASH

(V) Vegetarian (🌱) Vegan (🌾) Gluten free (👥) Serves 4 people

We love to roast squash as it really intensifies the flavour. We also always leave the skin on as it gives a sweet chewy texture. Great served with Moghul Spiced Lamb *(p. 110)*.

Ingredients

1 butternut squash

2 tbsp vegetable oil

½ tsp chilli flakes

½ tsp black pepper

½ tsp cumin seeds

½ tsp turmeric powder

1 tsp salt

Method

1. Preheat the oven to 190C/gas 5.
2. Chop the butternut squash into chunks, leaving the skin on.
3. Grind the spices in a pestle and mortar.
4. Mix the oil, spices and butternut squash together until well coated.
5. Tip onto a roasting tray and roast for 45-50 minutes, until the edges of the squash are crisp.

ROAST TOMATOES

(V) Vegetarian (🌱) Vegan (🌾) Gluten free (👥) Serves 4 people

Since discovering pul biber chilli flakes, we can't get enough. Breakfast will never be the same again!

Ingredients

6 tomatoes

1 tbsp olive oil

2 tsp of pul biber chilli flakes

1 tsp salt

1 tsp sugar

Method

1. Slice the tomatoes in half and place them face up on a roasting tray.

2. Drizzle the oil over the tomatoes and then sprinkle on the chilli, salt and sugar.

3. Roast in the oven at gas mark 160C/gas 3 for 40 minutes.

Top Tip:
Pul biber is a Turkish chilli flake which is quite mild, sweet and fruity. Any other chilli flakes would work, but be careful of the heat.

VEG

SPICED MASHED POTATOES

 V Vegetarian Vegan Gluten free Serves 4 people

"This mash is great to serve alongside anything, especially sausages! I originally wrote this recipe as a filling for the vada pavs *(p. 83)*, but it turned out so well, I'd happily eat it on its own." — *Hana*

Ingredients

2 tbsp vegetable oil

1 tsp mustard seeds

10 fresh curry leaves, sliced

1 inch ginger, peeled and grated

2 cloves garlic, finely chopped

2 chopped green chillies (or to taste)

½ tsp turmeric

¼ tsp asafoetida

½ tsp chaat masala *(p. 55)*

750g plain mashed potato

Salt to taste

Chopped fresh coriander to taste

Method

1. Heat the oil over medium heat, add mustard seeds and fry until they crackle.

2. Add curry leaves, ginger, garlic and chillies, frying for 10-20 seconds.

3. Take off the heat, add powdered spices and then tip spices and oil on top of the mashed potato.

4. Stir through with the fresh coriander and salt to taste.

Top Tip:
This is the perfect accompaniment to any of the fish recipes in this book!

CRUSHED SPICED PEAS

(V) Vegetarian   🌱 Vegan   🌾 Gluten free   👥 Serves 4 people

This recipe is perfect for when fresh garden peas are in season, but you can use frozen peas at any time. A fresh summery recipe, it is great served with fishcakes *(p. 98)*.

Ingredients

2 tbsp vegetable oil

10 fresh curry leaves, finely sliced

½ tsp mustard seeds

½ tsp onion seeds

Salt, to taste

500g peas

Large handful of fresh mint

Large handful of fresh coriander

Method

1. Heat the oil in a small frying pan. Add the mustard seeds, onion seeds and curry leaves. Cook for 2-3 minutes until the curry leaves have crisped up and the mustard seeds have started to pop.

2. Add the peas to the pan. Keep stirring until cooked to your liking.

3. Depending on the desired consistency you can either gently crush some of the peas with the back of a spoon, or blitz with a stick-blender, or leave the peas whole.

4. In a bowl, mix the peas with the mint and coriander.

5. Season with salt to taste before serving.

VEG

BUTTERED SPINACH AND ONION

(V) Vegetarian (※) Gluten free (👥) Serves 4 people

"This is comfort food at its most simple. Buttery onions and slightly spiced spinach makes a great, simple side to any meal on a chilly autumn or winter evening." — *Hana*

Ingredients

30g butter

1 large red onion, sliced thickly

1 inch ginger, finely chopped

½ tsp chilli powder

500g baby spinach

Salt

Method

1. Melt the butter in a pan and then fry the onions and ginger in the butter until soft.

2. Sprinkle over the chilli powder and stir well.

3. Add the spinach to the pan and stir gently until completely wilted.

4. Season to taste and serve.

BROCCOLI UPKARI

Upkari is a popular Konkani dish made by the people from coastal Karnataka and parts of Goa. Coconuts are abundant in this region and are a staple ingredient in many dishes. In this recipe the nutty, browned coconut works really well with the sweetness of the broccoli.

Ingredients

1 tbsp vegetable oil

½ tsp mustard seeds

½ tsp cumin seeds

1 dry red chilli, whole

1 fresh green chilli, sliced (or to taste)

1 clove garlic, sliced

250g broccoli (use heads and stems)

50ml water

Pinch salt

2 tbsp desiccated coconut

¼ tsp turmeric

Method

1. Heat the oil and fry the seeds until they crackle.

2. Add the garlic and the fresh and dry chillies.

3. Add the broccoli, water and salt and cook for 3-4 minutes until the broccoli is nearly done.

4. Add the desiccated coconut and the turmeric, stir well to combine and cook for 1 more minute.

5. Season to taste and serve.

VEG

163

DRINKS
&

SWEETS

These spiced sweet treats are ideal as mid- afternoon snacks or to finish off a fabulous feast. ∎

CARDAMOM BISCUITS

(V) Vegetarian (👥) Makes roughly 20 biscuits

Green cardamom is often used in sweets and drinks in India. We would always recommend buying it in small quantities, as it quickly loses its intense aroma.

Ingredients

125g butter, softened

90g soft dark brown sugar

2 tbsp golden syrup

200g self-raising flour

1 tsp ground cardamom seeds

Method

1. Preheat the oven to 200C/gas 6.

2. Cream the butter and sugar, beat in the syrup until fluffy, and then fold in the flour and cardamom.

3. Knead the dough until smooth, roll into a cylinder, wrap in cling film or parchment paper and place in the fridge for 15 minutes.

4. Remove from the fridge and cut into 5mm discs and place on a lightly greased baking tray leaving space between each biscuit.

5. Bake for 12-15 minutes. The biscuits should still be a little soft. Leave to cool and firm up.

Alternatives:
Sweet spices work best for these biscuits, try cinnamon, star anise or cloves.

CHAI (Spiced Tea)

Chai wallahs in India sell only chai tea and each one does something a little different to make themselves stand out. Some garnish with a strand of saffron, or a sprinkle of garam masala or add a special secret ingredient into their masala. This means that experimentation is positively encouraged! Play around with quantities and varieties of spices to find one that suits you.

Ingredients

For the masala:

4 black cardamom pods

8 green cardamom pods

2 inch cinnamon bark

2 tsp fennel seeds

10 cloves

1 tsp black peppercorns

For the tea:

700ml water

400ml milk

2 tsp black tea, such as Assam (tea bags are also fine)

3 or 4 thin slices of fresh ginger

Jaggery or demerara sugar, to taste (traditionally the tea is very sweet!)

Method

1. Dry toast the whole spices for the masala in a frying pan for 1-2 minutes (until you can smell them).

2. Bash them in a pestle and mortar, removing the outer shells of the cardamom pods once they have been cracked and keeping the seeds in the mix.

3. To make the chai: bring the water and the spices to the boil, adding more or less of the spice blend to taste (we tend to add the full amount). Add the milk, sugar and fresh ginger and bring the liquid to the boil again.

4. After simmering for 2 minutes, add the tea leaves or tea bags, simmer for a further two minutes then strain into 4 mugs. If you wish, add a whole star anise into each mug as a garnish.

Top Tip:
Jaggery is an unrefined palm sugar.

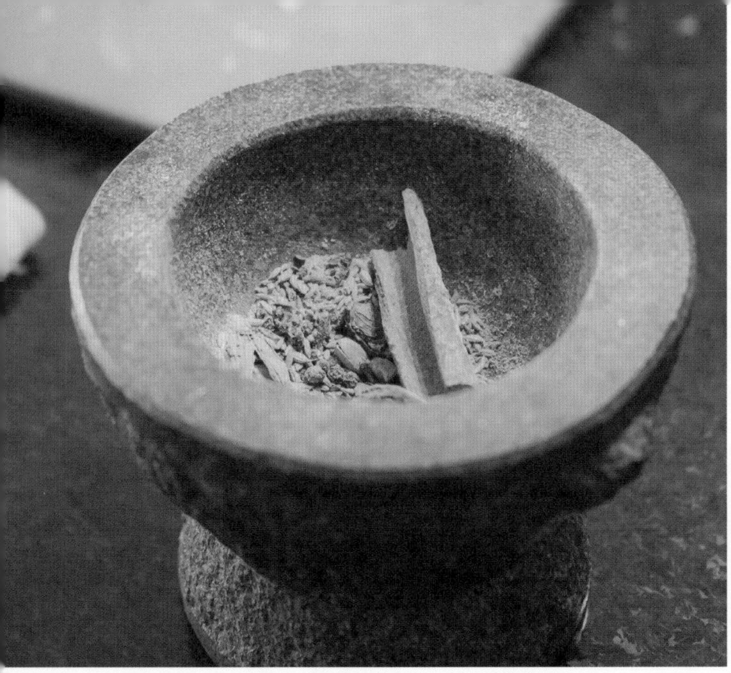

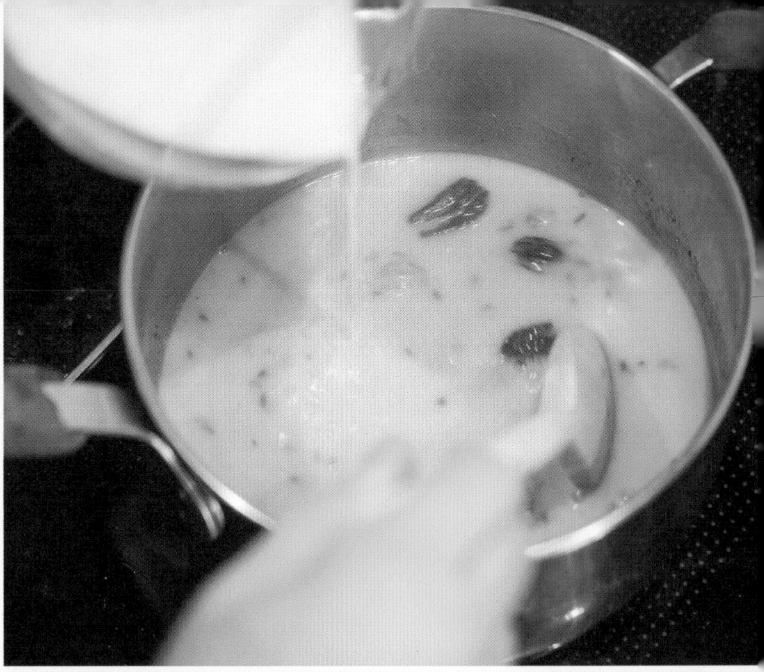

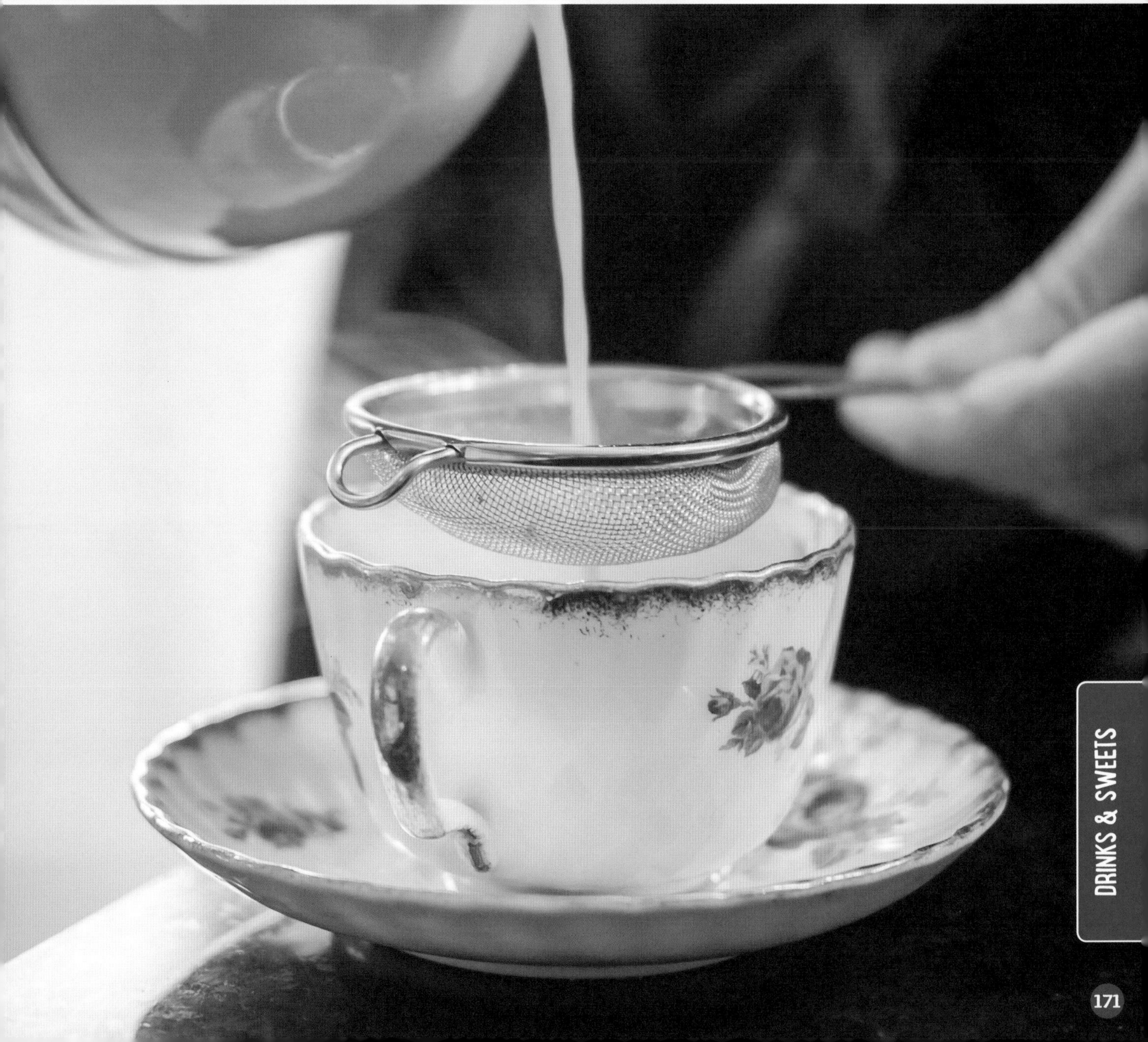

CHAI CHOCOLATE TRUFFLES

(V) Vegetarian (※) Gluten free (👥) Makes 12-15 truffles

These are lovely served with a coffee at the end of a dinner party or boxed up and given as gifts.

Ingredients

1 quantity of chai masala - left whole, do not grind (*p. 170*)

300ml double cream

30g salted butter

300g dark chocolate (ideally 70% or more)

Mix together: 5 tsp cocoa powder/grated chocolate and ½ tsp cinnamon powder

Method

1. Chop the dark chocolate and tip into a heat-proof bowl.
2. Gently heat the cream and whole spice masala mix in a saucepan for 10 minutes.
3. Tip the hot cream through a sieve over the chocolate and butter and whisk until combined.
4. Allow to chill in the fridge for 4 hours.
5. Shape the truffles and roll in the cocoa powder mix.

COURGETTE MUFFINS

"Perfect for the annual glut of courgettes! Courgettes keep muffins moist and delicious. They're not my favourite vegetable so I'm always looking for ways to jazz them up!" – *Lee*

The courgette can be replaced with carrot, or use both carrots and courgettes if you wish.

Ingredients

100g white self-raising flour

125g soft brown sugar

2 tsp mixed spice

½ tsp ground ginger

½ tsp baking powder

Pinch of salt

110g wholemeal self-raising flour

85g melted butter

180ml milk

1 egg, lightly beaten

175g courgette, grated

125g raisins

1 tsp demerara sugar

Method

1. Preheat the oven to 180C/gas 4.

2. Sieve together the white flour, sugar, mixed spice, ginger, salt and baking powder. Then sift in the wholemeal flour, keeping the larger bits of bran left in the sieve to one side for the topping.

3. Melt the butter, allow to cool, and then mix with the milk and egg.

4. Stir in the grated courgette, raisins and then the flour mixture.

5. Line a muffin tray with 12 paper cases.

6. Fill each one with the muffin mix till about two thirds full.

7. Mix together the reserved bran and demerara sugar and sprinkle on top of each muffin.

8. Bake for 25-30 minutes.

HANA'S MANGO SORBET

(V) Vegetarian (🌱) Vegan (🌾) Gluten free (👥) Serves 6-8 people

"This is very refreshing and perfect for a hot day! I like to serve it with a Mexican influence, by sprinkling it with chilli flakes, lime juice and finely shredded fresh mint." — *Hana*

Ingredients

1 tin of mango purée (850g)

680ml water

100g sugar

3 limes (zest and juice)

Method

1. Tip the mango purée into a wide bowl and place in the freezer to chill for 30 minutes.

2. Heat the sugar and the water in a saucepan, mixing until all of the sugar has dissolved. Set aside to cool.

3. Once the sugar syrup is completely cooled, add the lime juice and zest and whisk into the very cold mango purée until combined.

4. Put this back in the freezer. After one hour, remove from the freezer and whisk for 3-4 minutes. Repeat this twice more.

5. Serve plain, or sprinkled with chilli flakes and fresh mint.

KHEER (Rice Pudding)

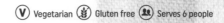 Vegetarian 🌾 Gluten free 🧑‍🤝‍🧑 Serves 6 people

This is a very traditional dish in India, often served at mosques and temples. It is very rich and sweet, as are most Indian deserts, so we suggest serving it in small portions along with some fresh or dried fruit to balance the sweetness.

Ingredients

25g butter

2 inch cinnamon bark

175g light brown sugar

115g long grain rice

2 pints whole milk

1 tsp ground cardamom

50g sultanas

25g flaked almonds

½ tsp freshly grated nutmeg

Method

1. Melt the butter in a pan, add the rice, milk, cinnamon, sugar and cardamom heat gently.

2. Stir on a low heat for 20 minutes or until the rice is nearly cooked.

3. Add the sultanas and almonds and keep stirring to prevent the rice from sticking.

4. When the mixture has thickened serve either warm or cold with a final dusting of nutmeg and some dried or fresh fruit.

KULFI (Indian Ice Cream)

(V) Vegetarian (※) Gluten free (👥) Makes 6

Kulfi is India's version of ice cream - it differs from our standard ice cream as it is not churned. Kulfi is therefore richer and, as a result, much firmer. Remove from the freezer for a good 10 to 15 minutes before serving to allow it to soften slightly.

As it is very rich, it is best served in small portions at the end of a meal and works well with a fruit garnish and maybe some biscuits to add texture.

Ingredients

1.25l whole milk

6 cardamom pods

85g demerara sugar

Pinch of salt

Pinch of saffron

½ tsp rose water

Sunflower oil, to grease

40g pistachios, finely chopped

Method

1. Place the milk and cracked cardamom pods in a saucepan, and bring to the boil, stirring constantly.

2. Once boiled, turn the heat down and simmer gently until reduced to about a half of its original volume – about 650ml. Keep stirring occasionally so it doesn't catch. This can take about 3 hours, depending on the pan you use, so patience is required.

3. Once reduced, remove the cardamom pods, stir in the sugar, salt and saffron, and simmer for another 5 minutes then allow to cool.

4. Lightly grease 6 dariole moulds and sprinkle with the chopped pistachios. Add the remaining pistachios to the milk and then pour into the moulds.

5. Alternatively add most of the nuts to the milk and pour into a freezer-proof container and then garnish with the remaining nuts once frozen.

6. Freeze for at least 6 hours. To serve, remove from the freezer about 10 minutes beforehand and dip the moulds briefly into hot water to release the kulfi.

Alternatives:

Once mastered there are no limits to the flavour combinations you can use. Other spices that work well are cinnamon and star anise. Fruit is often used to flavour it instead of spices, the classic being mango, but when in season strawberries with black pepper is amazing.

MANGO LASSI

(V) Vegetarian (※) Gluten free (👥) Serves 10 people

Lassi is a lovely cooling drink, and when it is too hot to eat, lassi is often drunk instead of a meal. You can drink it before a meal, or afterwards instead of a pudding! This also makes a lovely breakfast smoothie.

Ingredients

1 tin of mango purée (850g)

500g tub natural live yoghurt

500g water (fill empty yoghurt tub with water to measure)

Method

1 Whisk together the mango, yoghurt and water. A stick blender works really well for this.

2 Pour in to glasses and enjoy!

Alternatives:

When cooking for friends I like to serve a savoury lassi in little shot glasses before dinner. Simply replace the mango with 1 tsp of toasted, ground cumin seeds and a pinch of salt, to taste. — *Lee*

SPICED POACHED PEARS

(V) Vegetarian   (🌱) Vegan   (🌾) Gluten free   (👥) Serves 4 people

These pears make a great dinner party dessert. Once cooked they can be stored in the fridge for a few days and can be eaten warm or cold. Best served with crème fraîche or ice-cream.

Ingredients

4 pears

3 star anise

2 inch cinnamon stick

1 large pinch saffron

Zest of 1 lemon

500ml water

125g sugar

Juice of 1 lemon

25g pistachios, roasted and coarsely chopped or crushed

Method

1. Peel the pears and place in a saucepan with the water to stop discolouring. Add the spices, lemon zest and sugar and bring to the boil.

2. Simmer gently for about 20 minutes, or until the pears are tender.

3. Remove the pears from the syrup and keep in a shallow bowl. Return the liquid to the heat and simmer gently to reduce to a thick syrupy texture.

4. Once thick, add the lemon juice and pour over the pears. Serve with a sprinkling of chopped pistachios and a drizzle of the reduced syrup along with some crème fraîche.

Top Tip:
This dish works well with any fruit that is good poached, such as apples or rhubarb. It is possible to also add a crumble topping to the dish and heat in the oven for a spiced fruit crumble.

DRINKS & SWEETS

SHRIKHAND
(Sweet Yoghurt Pudding)

 (V) Vegetarian (🌾) Gluten free (👥) Serves 4 people

Shrikhand means 'ambrosia of the gods', and after trying this saffron-infused dessert you'll see why! If you love mangoes, you can add some mango purée into this to make amrakhand (mango ambrosia of the gods).

Ingredients

Pinch saffron soaked in 1 tsp warmed milk

50g icing sugar

500g Greek yoghurt: drain off any liquid that has separated in the tub. If possible strain in a muslin cloth to get rid of as much liquid as you can.

¼ grated nutmeg

Generous pinch ground cardamom

Crushed nuts: hazelnuts, walnuts, pistachios, almonds. Together equal to roughly 1 tbsp, plus more to garnish

Fresh fruits for the topping: we like raspberries and blueberries

Method

1 Put a pinch of saffron into the warm milk and set aside to infuse.

2 Add the icing sugar into the yoghurt and beat with a whisk for roughly 2 minutes, or until it becomes light and well mixed.

3 Grate in the nutmeg and add the cardamom – both of these to taste but both are quite strong, so start with smaller quantities and add more as required.

4 Add the milk and saffron threads and stir through.

5 Chill in the fridge for a couple of hours.

6 When ready to serve, stir through the crushed nuts and add more nuts and/or fruit to garnish as you wish. You can also serve this with the cardamom biscuits *(p. 169)* for a very decadent dessert.

SPICED FRUIT

Fruit and spices complement each other really well – just think of cinnamon in an apple pie or mixed spice in all those lovely Christmas cakes! We've been doing it in Britain for centuries without realising it.

This is not a recipe but some general ideas to get you started. Spiced fruit makes a great snack or even a starter or pudding.

Ideas

Strawberries:
Go well with black pepper.

Pineapple, Mango and Watermelon:
Make a dip for chunks of fruit by mixing equal parts of sea salt and caster sugar with some chilli flakes (to taste). A wonderful mouthful that's simultaneously sweet, salty, spicy and juicy.

Nectarines and Peaches:
Mix sugar and ground cinnamon for a great sweet, warming dip.

Melon:
Sprinkle it with cayenne pepper or chilli flakes.

Watermelon:
Make into a salad with green chillies, lime juice, a pinch of salt and fresh coriander.

Mango:
Great with toasted cumin - try in a lassi or mango salad.

Apricots:
Try with roasted cumin or, if dried, poached in a cardamon-flavoured syrup.

Assorted Fruits:
In North India, fruits like papaya, banana, apple and pineapple can be found mixed with chaat masala which often contains chilli peppers, black salt, asafoetida and amchur (mango powder). The sweet, sour flavours of the chaat along with the addition of salt help enhance the flavour of the fruit.

COCKTAILS

During the course of writing the book, we experimented with various drinks to aid the creative process. These two were so good they deserved to be included. The first is a light summery drink and the second is inspired by a traditional winter warmer.

GIN AND COCONUT WATER

Ingredients

200ml coconut water

50ml gin (one Shot)

Generous squeeze of lime

½ tsp ginger juice (1 inch ginger, grated and squeezed)

½ tsp of runny honey

Thin twist of lime peel

Method

1. Combine the first five ingredients shaken with ice is best, pour in to a tumbler with fresh ice. Garnish with the lime peel and serve.

SPICED RUM OLD FASHIONED

Ingredients

25ml (one shot) Dark Rum

2 Dashes of angostura bitters

1 Sugar cube

Thin twist of orange peel

1 inch cinnamon stick toasted

1 star anise toasted

Method

1 Place sugar cube in tumbler and saturate with the angostura bitters, add a few drops of rum. Muddle until dissolved.

2 Fill the glass with ice and add the remaining rum, stir well. Twist the orange peel and add along with the spices to garnish.

INDEX

A

achar,
(Malaysian mixed vegetable pickle), 17
ajwain seed, 85
almonds,
kheer (rice pudding), 178
Moghul style roast lamb, 110
shrikhand (sweet yoghurt pudding), 186
vegetable pilau, 51
Alphonso Mango,
mango lassi, 182
mango sorbet, 177
aloo chaat, 55
amchur powder (mango powder),
aloo chaat, 55
asparagus dippers, boiled eggs
and spiced salts, 56
masala papads (papadums), 75
paneer tikka kebabs, 76
seekh kebab, 113
spiced fruit, 189
apple,
spiced poached pears, 185
asparagus,
asparagus dippers, boiled eggs
and spiced salts, 56
asparagus dippers, boiled eggs
and spiced salts, 56
aubergine,
aubergine and coconut fry, 119
aviyal (coconut and vegetable broth), 120
aubergine and coconut fry, 119
aviyal (coconut and vegetable broth), 120

B

baked stuffed fish, 89
barbecue,
barbecue sweetcorn with lime
and chaat, 59
chutney chicken, 94
grilled lamb chops, 102
paneer tikka kebabs, 76
prawn kebab, 109
seekh kebab, 113
barbecue sweetcorn with lime and chaat, 59

basmati rice,
coconut rice, 28
lemon rice, 32
plain rice, 40
South Indian tomato rice, 48
vegetable pilau, 51
beef,
beef fry, 90
kheema (mince curry), 105
koftas (spiced meatballs), 106
beef fry, 90
kati rolls, 71
beetroot,
beetroot curry, 123
beetroot pickle, 18
beetroot curry, 123
beetroot pickle, 18
Bengali,
cherry tomato chutney, 23
tomatoes on toast, 68
bhel puri, 60
black dhal (lentil),
dhal makhani, 135
boiled egg curry, 127
koftas (spiced meatballs), 106
Bombay mix,
aloo chaat, 55
bhel puri, 60
bread,
kati rolls, 71
masala omelette, 72
seekh kebab, 113
spiced squash soup, 80
tomatoes on toast, 68
breads,
chapati flatbreads, 20
naan breads, 34
parathas, 36
stuffed parathas, 44
vada pav (mashed potato burger), 83
breadcrumbs,
spiced fish cakes, 98
bread flour,
naan breads, 34
broccoli,
upkari, 163

INDEX

brussels sprouts,
brussels sprouts and ajwain, *127*
brussels sprouts and ajwain, *127*
butter,
buttered spinach and onion, *160*
cardamom biscuits, *169*
chai chocolate truffles, *173*
dhal makhani, *135*
buttered spinach and onion, *160*
butternut squash,
roast squash, *152*
spiced squash soup, *80*

C

cabbage,
achar (Malaysian mixed
vegetable pickle), *17*
cabbage and egg scramble, *130*
kati rolls, *71*
red cabbage slaw, *148*
stuffed parathas, *44*
cabbage and egg scramble, *130*
canapé,
masala papads (papadums), *75*
cardamom, *85*
cardamom biscuits, *169*
chai, *170*
kheer (rice pudding), *178*
kulfi (Indian ice cream), *181*
shrikhand (sweet yoghurt pudding), *186*
cardamom biscuits, *169*
shrikhand (sweet yoghurt pudding), *186*
carrot,
achar (Malaysian mixed
vegetable pickle), *17*
aviyal (coconut and vegetable
broth), *120*
carrot salad, *132*
chickpea chaat salad, *63*
vegetable pilau, *51*
carrot salad, *132*
kati rolls, *71*
koftas (spiced meatballs), *106*
seekh kebab, *113*

cashew nuts,
coconut rice, *28*
lemon rice, *32*
vegetable pilau, *51*
cauliflower,
achar (Malaysian mixed vegetable
pickle), *17*
spiced roast cauliflower, *151*
vegetable pilau, *51*
chaat masala, *55*
aloo chaat, *55*
barbecue sweetcorn with
lime and chaat, *59*
bhel puri, *60*
paneer tikka kebabs, *76*
spiced fruit, *189*
spiced mashed potatoes, *156*
chai, *170*
chai chocolate truffles, *173*
chai masala,
chai, *170*
chai chocolate truffles, *173*
chana dhal (lentil),
coconut rice, *28*
lemon rice, *32*
South Indian tomato rice, *48*
tarka dhal, *144*
chapati flatbreads, *20*
beetroot curry, *123*
kati rolls, *71*
kheema (mince curry), *105*
Moghul style roast lamb, *110*
potatoes in hot red sauce, *143*
chapati flour,
chapati flatbreads, *20*
parathas, *36*
stuffed parathas, *44*
cherry tomato chutney, *23*
chicken,
chicken curry, *93*
chutney chicken, *94*
kati rolls, *71*
Moghul style roast lamb, *110*
tamarind salmon, *114*
chicken curry, *93*
curry puffs, *67*

INDEX

chickpea,
  aloo chaat, *55*
  chickpea chaat salad, *63*
chickpea chaat salad, *63*
chilli sambal, *24*
  beef fry, *90*
  kati rolls, *71*
  vada pav (mashed potato burger), *83*
chillies, *85*
  chilli sambal, *24*
chai masala,
  chai, *170*
  chai chocolate truffles, *173*
Chinese five spice,
  beef fry, *90*
  chicken curry, *93*
chocolate,
  chai chocolate truffles, *173*
chopped salad (kachoombar), *139*
chutney,
  bhel puri, *60*
  cherry tomato chutney, *23*
  chickpea chaat salad, *63*
  chutney chicken, *94*
  coconut chutney, *27*
  potatoes in hot red sauce, *143*
  tamarind salmon, *114*
  vada pav (mashed potato burger), *83*
chutney chicken, *94*
  kati rolls, *71*
cinnamon bark, *85*
cocktails, *190*
coconut chutney, *27*
coconut cream,
  chicken curry, *93*
  coconut rice, *28*
coconut, desiccated,
  aubergine and coconut fry, *119*
  aviyal (coconut and vegetable broth), *120*
  beef fry, *90*
  boiled egg curry, *127*
  coconut chutney, *27*
  coriander chutney, *31*
  spiced squash soup, *80*
  upkari broccoli, *163*

coconut milk,
  beetroot curry, *123*
coconut oil,
  aviyal (coconut and vegetable broth), *120*
  beef fry, *90*
  coconut rice, *28*
  South Indian fish fry, *97*
coconut rice, *28*
coriander chutney, *31*
  baked stuffed fish, *89*
  bhel puri, *60*
  grilled lamb chops, *102*
  kati rolls, *71*
  vada pav (mashed potato burger), *83*
coriander, fresh,
  bhel puri, *60*
  chickpea chaat salad, *63*
  coconut chutney, *27*
  coriander chutney, *31*
  curry puffs, *67*
  crushed spiced peas, *159*
  koftas (spiced meatballs), *106*
  masala omelette, *72*
  masala papads (papadums), *75*
  pickled onions, *38*
  spiced fruit, *189*
  spiced mashed potatoes, *156*
coriander seed, *85*
courgette,
  courgette curry, *124*
  courgette kofta, *64*
  courgette muffins, *175*
courgette curry, *124*
courgette kofta, *64*
  kadhi (yogurt curry), *140*
courgette muffins, *175*
cream,
  chai chocolate truffles, *173*
  dhal makhani, *135*
crushed spiced peas, *159*
  spiced fish cakes, *98*
cucumber,
  achar (Malaysian mixed vegetable pickle), *17*
  aloo chaat, *55*

INDEX

aviyal (coconut and vegetable broth), *120*

kachoombar (chopped salad), *139*

cumin seed, *85*

cumin lassi, *182*

curry,

beetroot curry, *123*

boiled egg curry, *127*

curry puffs, *67*

chicken curry, *93*

courgette curry, *132*

kheema (mince curry), *105*

koftas (spiced meatballs), *106*

Curry Packs,

vada pav (mashed potato burger), *83*

curry paste,

chicken curry, *93*

kheema (mince curry), *105*

curry puffs, *67*

chicken curry, *93*

kheema (mince curry), *105*

D

dhal (lentil),

dhal makhani, *135*

rasam (tomato and lentil soup), *79*

tarka dhal, *144*

dhal makhani, *135*

E

eggs,

asparagus dippers, boiled eggs and spiced salts, *56*

boiled egg curry, *127*

cabbage and egg scramble, *130*

kati rolls, *71*

masala omelette, *72*

spiced fish cakes, *98*

F

flatbreads, *20*

fish,

baked stuffed fish, *89*

prawn kebab, *109*

South Indian fish fry, *97*

spiced fish cakes, *98*

tamarind salmon, *114*

fruit,

kheer (rice pudding), *178*

kulfi (Indian ice cream), *181*

shrikhand (sweet yoghurt pudding), *186*

spiced fruit, *189*

G

garam masala, *85*

beef fry, *90*

cabbage and egg scramble, *130*

chai, *170*

courgette curry, *132*

courgette kofta, *64*

dhal makhani, *135*

Goan pork pickle, *101*

grilled lamb chops, *102*

koftas (spiced meatballs), *106*

masala omelette, *72*

Moghul style roast lamb, *110*

paneer tikka kebabs, *76*

seekh kebab, *113*

South Indian fish fry, *97*

spiced squash soup, *80*

vegetable pilau, *51*

gin,

gin and coconut water cocktail, *190*

gin and coconut water cocktail, *190*

Goa,

Goan pork pickle, *101*

prawn kebab, *109*

upkari broccoli, *163*

Goan pork pickle, *101*

gram flour,

boiled egg curry, *127*

courgette kofta, *64*

kadhi (yogurt curry), *140*

pudlas (gram flour pancakes), *43*

vada pav (mashed potato burger), *83*

Greek yoghurt,

shrikhand (sweet yoghurt pudding), *186*

green beans,

spiced green beans, *136*

vegetable pilau, *51*

grilled lamb chops, *102*

Gujarati,

pudlas (gram flour pancakes), *43*

INDEX

I

Indian Vegetarian Cookery,
    tarka yoghurt, *47*

J

jaggery, *170*
    chai, *170*
    cherry tomato chutney, *23*
    potatoes in hot red sauce, *143*

K

kachoombar (chopped salad), *139*
kadhi (yoghurt curry), *140*
    courgette kofta, *64*
Kashmiri Chillies, *76*
    paneer tikka kebabs, *76*
    potatoes in hot red sauce, *143*
Kashmiri Chilli powder,
    paneer tikka kebabs, *76*
    seekh kebab, *113*
kati rolls, *71*
    beef fry, *90*
Kerala,
    coconut chutney, *27*
    prawn kebab, *109*
kheema (mince curry), *105*
    curry puffs, *67*
    stuffed parathas, *44*
kheer (rice pudding), *178*
kidney beans,
    dhal makhani, *135*
koftas (spiced meatballs), *106*
Kolkata,
    kati rolls, *71*
kulfi (Indian ice cream), *181*

L

lal batata (potatoes in hot red sauce), *143*
lamb,
    grilled lamb chops, *102*
    kheema (mince curry), *105*
    koftas (spiced meatballs), *106*
    Moghul style roast lamb, *110*
    seekh kebab, *113*

leftovers,
    curry puffs, *67*
    kheema (mince curry), *105*
    stuffed parathas, *44*
lemon rice, *32*
lentil,
    coconut chutney, *27*
    coconut rice, *28*
    dhal makhani, *135*
    rasam (tomato and lentil soup), *79*
    tarka dhal, *144*
lime,
    barbecue sweetcorn with lime
    and chaat, *59*
    gin and coconut water cocktail, *190*
    mango sorbet, *177*
    tamarind salmon, *114*
    spiced green beans, *136*
long grain rice,
    kheer (rice pudding), *178*

M

mackerel,
    South Indian fish fry, *97*
Malaysia,
    spiced fish cakes, *98*
Malaysian Cookery, *17*
mango,
    kulfi (Indian ice cream), *181*
    mango lassi, *182*
    mango sorbet, 177
    spiced fruit, *189*
mango lassi, *182*
mango powder (amchur powder),
    aloo chaat, *55*
    asparagus dippers, boiled eggs
    and spiced salts, *56*
    masala papads (papadums), *75*
    paneer tikka kebabs, *76*
    seekh kebab, *113*
    spiced fruit, *189*
mango sorbet, *177*
masala dabba, *85*
masala omelette, *72*
masala papads (papadums), *75*
masoor dhal,
    tarka dhal, *144*

INDEX

melon,
> spiced fruit, *189*

milk,
> chai, *170*
> courgette muffins, *175*
> kheer (rice pudding), *178*
> kulfi (Indian ice cream), *181*
> naan breads, *34*
> shrikhand (sweet yoghurt pudding), *186*

mint, fresh,
> aloo chaat, *55*
> baked stuffed fish, *89*
> coriander chutney, *31*
> crushed spiced peas, *159*
> grilled lamb chops, *102*
> koftas (spiced meatballs), *106*
> mango sorbet, *177*

mixed spice,
> courgette muffins, *175*

mixed vegetables,
> achar (Malaysian mixed vegetable pickle), *17*
> aviyal (coconut and vegetable broth), *120*
> vegetable pilau, *51*

Moghul style roast lamb, *110*

Mumbai,
> vada pav (mashed potato burger), *83*

mustard seed, *85*

Mysore,
> coconut chutney, *27*

N

naan breads, *34*

nuts,
> achar (Malaysian mixed vegetable pickle), *17*
> chai chocolate truffles, *173*
> coconut rice, *28*
> kheer (rice pudding), *178*
> kulfi (Indian ice cream), *181*
> lemon rice, *32*
> okra fry, *147*
> shrikhand (sweet yoghurt pudding), *186*
> vegetable pilau, *51*

O

okra,
> okra fry, *147*

okra fry, *147*

onion,
> buttered spinach and onion, *160*
> kachoombar (chopped salad), *139*
> pickled onions, *38*
> red cabbage slaw, *148*

onion seeds, *85*

P

panch pooran, *23*
> cherry tomato chutney, *23*
> tomatoes on toast, *68*

paneer,
> paneer tikka kebabs, *76*
> kati rolls, *71*

paneer tikka kebabs, *76*

papads (papadums),
> masala papads (papadums), *75*

parathas, *36*
> cabbage and egg scramble, *130*
> kati rolls, *71*

Parsi,
> baked stuffed fish, *89*
> kachoombar (chopped salad), *139*

passata,
> kheema (mince curry), *105*
> rasam (tomato and lentil soup), *79*

peanuts,
> achar (Malaysian mixed vegetable pickle), *17*
> aloo chaat, *55*
> lemon rice, *32*
> okra fry, *147*

pears,
> spiced poached pears, *185*

peas,
> aviyal (coconut and vegetable broth), *120*
> spiced fish cakes, *98*
> crushed spiced peas, *159*
> kheema (mince curry), *105*

INDEX

peppers,
kachoombar (chopped salad), *139*
paneer tikka kebabs, *76*
Peshwari naan,
naan breads, *34*
pickle,
achar (Malaysian mixed
vegetable pickle), *17*
beetroot pickle, *18*
chilli sambal, *24*
Goan pork pickle, *101*
pickled onions, *38*
pickled onions, *38*
pilau rice,
plain rice, *40*
pineapple,
kulfi (Indian ice cream), *181*
spiced fruit, *189*
pistachios,
kulfi (Indian ice cream), *181*
spiced poached pears, *185*
shrikhand (sweet yoghurt pudding), *186*
plain rice, *40*
rasam (tomato and lentil soup), *79*
poppy seeds,
boiled egg curry, *127*
pork,
Goan pork pickle, *101*
potatoes,
aloo chaat, *55*
bhel puri, *60*
curry puffs, *67*
potatoes in hot red sauce, *143*
spiced fish cakes, *98*
spiced mashed potatoes, *156*
spiced roast cauliflower, *151*
potatoes in hot red sauce, *143*
prawn kebab, *109*
prawns,
kati rolls, *71*
prawn kebab, *109*
pudlas (gram flour pancakes), *43*
puff pastry,
curry puffs, *67*
pul biber chilli flake, *155*
beetroot pickle, *18*
roast tomatoes, *155*

Punjabi,
dhal makhani, *135*

R

radish,
kachoombar (chopped salad), *139*
raisins,
courgette muffins, *175*
raita,
baked stuffed fish, *89*
coriander chutney, *31*
South Indian tomato rice, *48*
Ramadan,
vegetable pilau, *51*
rasam (tomato and lentil soup), *79*
red cabbage slaw, *148*
kati rolls, *71*
red lentils,
rasam (tomato and lentil soup), *79*
tarka dhal, *144*
rhubarb,
spiced poached pears, *185*
rice,
coconut rice, *28*
kheer (rice pudding), *178*
lemon rice, *32*
plain rice, *40*
South Indian tomato rice, *48*
vegetable pilau, *51*
roast squash, *152*
roast tomatoes, *155*
rose water,
kulfi (Indian ice cream), *181*
rum,
spiced rum Old Fashioned, *190*

S

saffron,
kulfi (Indian ice cream), *181*
plain rice, *40*
spiced poached pears, *185*
shrikhand (sweet yoghurt
pudding), *186*
salads,
carrot salad, *132*
chickpea chaat salad, *63*

INDEX

kachoombar (chopped salad), *139*

red cabbage slaw, 148

salmon,

South Indian fish fry, *97*

tamarind salmon, *114*

seekh kebab, *113*

sesame oil,

boiled egg curry, *127*

sesame seeds,

achar (Malaysian mixed vegetable pickle), *17*

boiled egg curry, *127*

shrikhand (sweet yoghurt pudding), *186*

soup,

rasam (tomato and lentil soup), *79*

spiced squash soup, *80*

South India,

aviyal (coconut and vegetable broth), *120*

coconut chutney, *27*

coconut rice, *28*

plain rice, *40*

rasam (tomato and lentil soup), *79*

South Indian fish fry, *97*

South Indian tomato rice, *48*

tarka yoghurt, *47*

South Indian fish fry, *97*

South Indian tomato rice, *48*

spice box, *84*

spiced fish cakes, *98*

crushed spiced peas, *159*

spiced fruit, *189*

spiced green beans, *136*

spiced mashed potatoes, *156*

curry puffs, *67*

kheema (mince curry), *105*

stuffed parathas, *44*

vada pav (mashed potato burger), *83*

spiced poached pears, *185*

spiced roast cauliflower, *151*

spiced rum Old Fashioned, *190*

spiced salts, *56*

spiced squash soup, *80*

spinach,

buttered spinach and onion, *160*

parathas, *36*

squash,

potatoes in hot red sauce, *143*

roast squash, *152*

spiced squash soup, *80*

Sri Lanka,

beetroot curry, *123*

star anise, *85*

strawberries,

kulfi (Indian ice cream), *181*

spiced fruit, *189*

stuffed parathas, *44*

sultanas,

kheer (rice pudding), *178*

naan breads, *34*

sweetcorn,

barbecue sweetcorn with lime and chaat, *59*

vegetable pilau, *51*

sweet yoghurt pudding (shrikhand), *186*

T

tamarind,

potatoes in hot red sauce, *143*

rasam (tomato and lentil soup), *79*

tamarind chutney,

aloo chaat, *55*

bhel puri, *60*

chickpea chaat salad, *63*

chutney chicken, *94*

tamarind salmon, *114*

vada pav (mashed potato burger), *83*

tamarind salmon, *114*

tarka, *47*

kadhi (yoghurt curry), *140*

spiced squash soup, *80*

tarka dhal, *144*

tarka yoghurt, *47*

tarka dhal, *144*

tarka yoghurt, *47*

tea,

chai, *170*

tomato,

aloo chaat, *55*

bhel puri, *60*

boiled egg curry, *127*

cherry tomato chutney, *23*

INDEX

courgette curry, *132*
kachoombar (chopped salad), *139*
masala omelette, *72*
masala papads (papadums), *75*
rasam (tomato and lentil soup), *79*
roast tomatoes, *155*
tomatoes on toast, *68*
South Indian tomato rice, *48*
tomatoes on toast, 68
toor dhal,
tarka dhal, *144*
turmeric, 85

U

upkari, *163*
urid dhal,
coconut chutney, *27*
coconut rice, *28*
dhal makhani, *135*
lemon rice, *32*
South Indian tomato rice, *48*

V

vada pav (mashed potato burger), *83*
chilli sambal, *24*
coconut chutney, *27*
coriander chutney, *31*
spiced mashed potatoes, *156*
vegetable pilau, *51*
vinegar,
achar (Malaysian mixed vegetable pickle), *17*
beef fry, *90*
beetroot pickle, *18*
cherry tomato chutney, *23*
chilli sambal, *24*
Goan pork pickle, *101*
pickled onions, *38*

W

watermelon,
spiced fruit, *189*

Y

yeast,
naan breads, *34*
yoghurt,
aloo chaat, *55*
aviyal (coconut and vegetable broth), *120*
bhel puri, *60*
chutney chicken, *94*
coriander chutney, *31*
courgette kofta, *64*
kadhi (yoghurt curry), *140*
kati rolls, *71*
koftas (spiced meatballs), *106*
mango lassi, *182*
Moghul style roast lamb, *110*
naan breads, *34*
paneer tikka kebabs, *76*
seekh kebab, *113*
shrikhand (sweet yoghurt pudding), *186*
tarka yoghurt, *47*
spiced fruit, *189*
yoghurt curry (kadhi), *140*

Saturday night

Kheema
Chapatis ✓
Kachoombar
Dhal ✓

YOUR
NOTES

Acknowledgements

There are so many people who have contributed to the book so a heartfelt thank you to everyone for your support and guidance, including all of our wonderful customers over the past 30 years.

An enormous thank you to the fantastic team at the Spicebox, both past and present. They are truly the most important part of the business and have all helped the book along the way with research, proof reading, cooking and an awful lot of tasting. The most passionate group of foodies we could hope for.

In particular, a special mention to Ian and Hana, our senior team; their enthusiasm, commitment and creative vision are unrivalled and this book is a real testament to their knowledge of food and dedication to the Spicebox.

Jim Poyner, our photographer, created the most beautiful photos to show off our food and was brilliant to work with. Most of the photos were taken over an intense four days of cooking every dish and they are amazing; a true representation of our recipes and our love of sharing food with friends and family.

Thanks to the team at Press Green, our design team, who created all the page layouts. Special mention to Andrew and Adam whose creativity and ideas never cease to amaze us. We have worked with them both for many years and they absolutely 'get us' and everything we are aiming for.

Thank you to the team at York Publishing Services, especially Duncan and Dave, who are not only great neighbours but have also produced a beautiful-looking book that has made us all incredibly proud.

Finally a huge thank you to the Fernandez family: Rafi, Den, Lee and Tanya as well our extended family in India, Malaysia and UK. This book is a result of over 30 years of continued hard work. A special mention has to go to my wife, Donna, and daughter, Lily, for their patience and support for me and all of us at the Spicebox. We wouldn't have got here without you.